how to

Teach

Grammar

Scott Thornbury

Longman

series editor:
Jeremy Harmer

Pearson Education Limited
Edinburgh Gate
Harlow
Essex CM20 2JE
England
and Associated Companies thoughout the World

www.longman.com

First published 1999
Ninth impression 2006
Printed in Malaysia, PP

Produced for the publishers by Bluestone Press, Charlbury, Oxfordshire, UK
Text design by Keith Rigley at White Horse Graphics

ISBN-13: 978-0-582-33932-3
ISBN-10: 0-582-33932-4

Acknowledgements
We are grateful to the following for permission to reproduce copyright material: British National Corpus for extracts based on headings 'Remember', 'Forget' and 'Stop' from *The British National Corpus* web site; Cambridge University Press and the author for an extract from *English Grammar in Use* by R. Murphy (1994); Oxford University Press for an extract and illustration from *Oxford Progressive English Course* by Hornby (1954); Pearson Education Ltd for extracts and illustrations from *Over to Us*, *ESO 4*, Teacher's Book by Palencia and Thornbury published by Longman Group Ltd (1998) and from *Grammar Practice for Intermediate Students* by Walker & Elsworth published by Longman Group Ltd (1986).

We have been unable to trace the copyright holder of news items 'Concern for missing monkey', 'Sighting of missing monkey', 'Monkey still on the loose', 'Escaped monkey shot dead' from *TVNZ* web site (1997), and would appreciate any information which would enable us to do so.

Illustrations on page 106 by Roy Nixon

For Kate
Sastipén ta mistipén!

Contents

Acknowledgements

The following colleagues and friends may recognise bits of themselves scattered throughout this book – to them many thanks: Jessica MacKay, Lynn Durrant, Nicole Taylor, Theresa Zanatta, Karl Kaliski, Piet Luethi, Neil Forrest, and Albert Stahl. Thanks are also due to Jeremy Harmer, for his boundless enthusiasm from start to finish, and to Hester Lott, for her skilful and painstaking editing.

I also wish to acknowledge the help and inspiration that three books have given me: Peter Skehan's *A Cognitive Approach to Language Learning* (Oxford University Press, 1998); Rod Ellis's *SLA Research and Language Teaching* (Oxford University Press, 1997); and Keith Johnson's *Language Teaching and Skill Learning* (Blackwell, 1996). I should, of course, add that no blame must be attached to those books for any flaws in this one.

Introduction

Who is this book for?

How to Teach Grammar has been written for teachers of English who are curious or confused or unconvinced about the teaching of grammar. They may be in training, relatively new to the job, or very experienced.

What is this book about?

Grammar teaching has always been one of the most controversial and least understood aspects of language teaching. Few teachers remain indifferent to grammar and many teachers become obsessed by it. This book attempts to shed light on the issues, but it is essentially a book about practice, about *how*, and the bulk of the book explores a range of grammar teaching options.

Chapter 1 contains a brief overview of what grammar is, and Chapter 2 addresses the pros and cons of grammar instruction.

The sample lessons that comprise the rest of the book have been chosen both to represent a range of teaching approaches, and also as vehicles for the teaching of a representative selection of grammar items – the sort of items that any current coursebook series will include. Each sample lesson is followed by a discussion of the rationale underpinning it, and an evaluation of it according to criteria that are established in Chapter 2. It is important to bear in mind that each lesson description is simply that: a description. The lessons are not meant to represent an ideal way of teaching grammar: there are as many different ways of teaching grammar as there are teachers teaching it, and it is not the purpose of this book to promote any one particular method or approach over another. Rather, the purpose is to trigger cycles of classroom experimentation and reflection, taking into account the features of every individual teaching situation. As the Rule of Appropriacy (see Chapter 10) puts it: Interpret any suggestions according to the level, needs, interests, expectations and learning styles of your students. This may mean giving a lot of prominence to grammar, or it may mean never actually teaching grammar – in an up-front way – at all.

The Task File at the back of the book comprises a number of tasks relevant to each chapter. They can be used as a basis for discussion in a training context, or for individual reflection and review. A Key is provided for those tasks that expect specific answers.

What is grammar?

- Texts, sentences, words, sounds
- Grammar and meaning
- Two kinds of meaning
- Grammar and function
- Spoken grammar and written grammar
- Grammar syllabuses
- Grammar rules

Texts, sentences, words, sounds

Here is an example of language in use:

> This is 2680239. We are not at home right now. Please leave a message after the beep.

You will recognise it as an answerphone message. That is the kind of **text** it is. It consists of three **sentences**, which themselves consist of **words**, and the words (when spoken) consist of **sounds**. All language in use can be analysed at each of these four levels: text, sentence, word and sound. These are the **forms** that language takes. The study of grammar consists, in part, of looking at the way these forms are arranged and patterned.

For example, if you change the order of the sentences you no longer have a well-formed answerphone message:

> Please leave a message after the beep. This is 2680239. We are not at home right now.

Likewise, the order of words in each sentence is fairly fixed:

> Beep after a leave the please message.

The same applies to the order of sounds in a word:

> peeb

Grammar is partly the study of what forms (or structures) are possible in a language. Traditionally, grammar has been concerned almost exclusively with analysis at the level of the sentence. Thus a grammar is a description of the rules that govern how a language's sentences are formed. Grammar attempts to explain why the following sentences are acceptable:

> We are not at home right now.
> Right now we are not at home.

but why this one is not:

> Not we at right home now are.

Nor this one:

> We is not at home right now.

The system of rules that cover the order of words in a sentence is called **syntax**. Syntax rules disallow:

> Not we at right home now are.

The system of rules that cover the formation of words is called **morphology**. Morphology rules disallow:

> We is not at home right now.

Grammar is conventionally seen as the study of the syntax and morphology of sentences. Put another way, it is the study of linguistic **chains** and **slots**. That is, it is the study both of the way words are chained together in a particular order, and also of what kinds of words can slot into any one link in the chain. These two kinds of relation can be shown diagrammatically:

1	2	3	4	5
We	are	not	at	home.
They	are		at	work.
Dad	is		in	hospital.
I	am		in	bed.

Notice that the order of elements on the horizontal axis is fairly fixed. The effect of switching the first two columns has a major effect on meaning: it turns the sentence into a question: *Are we not at home? Is Dad in bed?* Switching columns two and three, or four and five, is simply not possible. Similarly, it should be clear that the elements in the first column share a noun-like function, those in the second column fill the verb slot and those in the fourth column are prepositions. Again, it is not possible to take slot-filling elements and make chains of them. *We are not at home work bed* does not work as an English sentence.

It is the capacity to recognise the constraints on how sentence elements are chained and on how sentence slots are filled that makes a good amateur grammarian. For example, different languages have different constraints on the way chains are ordered and slots are filled. Many second language learner errors result from overgeneralising rules from their own language. So, in:

> I want that your agency return me the money.

the learner has selected the wrong kind of chain to follow the verb *want*. While in:

> I have chosen to describe Stephen Hawking, a notorious scientific of our century.

the chain is all right, but the words chosen to fill certain slots don't fit. *Notorious* has the wrong shade of meaning, while *scientific* is an adjective wrongly inserted into a noun slot.

From a learner's perspective, the ability both to recognise and to produce well-formed sentences is an essential part of learning a second language. But there are a number of problems. First, as we shall see, there is a great deal of debate as to how this ability is best developed. Second, it is not entirely clear what 'well-formed' really means, when a lot of naturally occurring speech seems to violate strict grammatical rules. For example, in many English-speaking contexts *We ain't at home* would be preferred to *We are not at home* yet only the latter has made it into the grammar books.

Third, an exclusive focus on sentences, rather than on texts or on words, risks under-equipping the learner for real language use. There is more to language learning than the ability to produce well-formed sentences. Texts and words also have grammar, in the sense that there are rules governing how both texts and words are organised, but it is not always clear where sentence grammar ends and either word grammar or text grammar begins. But, since most language teaching coursebooks and grammars are still firmly grounded in the sentence grammar tradition, for the purposes of this book we will assume grammar to mean grammar at the level of the sentence.

Grammar and meaning

In the last section the point was made that 'grammar is partly the study of what forms are possible'. But that does not explain why the following sounds odd:

This is 2680239. We are at home right now. Please leave a message after the beep.

The sentence *We are at home right now* is possible. That is, it is grammatically well-formed. But it doesn't make sense in this context. The form the speaker has chosen doesn't convey the exact meaning the speaker requires. We now need to consider another feature of grammar, and that is, its meaning-making potential.

Grammar communicates meanings – meanings of a very precise kind. Vocabulary, of course, also communicates meanings. Take this example: a ticket inspector on a train says:

Tickets!

Here there is little or no grammar – in the sense of either morphology or syntax. The meaning is conveyed simply at the **lexical**, or word level, *tickets*. Situational factors – such as the passengers' expectation that the inspector will want to check their tickets – mean that the language doesn't have to work very hard to make the meaning clear. The language of early childhood is like this: it is essentially individual words strung together, but because it is centred in the here-and-now, it is generally not difficult to interpret:

Carry!
All gone milk!
Mummy book.
Where daddy?

Adult language, too, is often pared down, operating on a lexical level (i.e. without much grammar):

A: Coffee?
B: Please.
A: Milk?
B: Just a drop.

We can formulate a rule of thumb: the more context, the less grammar. *Tickets!* is a good example of this. But imagine a situation when a person (Milly) is phoning another person (Molly) to ask a third person (Mandy) to forward some pre-booked airline tickets. In this case, *Tickets!* would be inadequate. Instead, we would expect something like:

Can you ask Mandy to send me the tickets that I booked last week?

This is where grammar comes in. Grammar is a process for making a speaker's or writer's meaning clear when contextual information is lacking. Baby talk is fine, up to a point, but there soon comes a time when we want to express meanings for which simple words are not enough. To do this we employ rules of syntax and rules of morphology and map these on to the meaning-carrying words, so that *Mummy book*, for example, becomes (according to the meaning the child wants to convey):

That's Mummy's book.

or:

Mummy's got a book.

or:

Mummy, give me the book.

Language learners have to make do with a period of baby-like talk and reliance on contextual clues, until they have enough grammar to express and understand a greater variety of meanings. Depending on their vocabulary knowledge and their resourcefulness, they can often cope surprisingly well. However, they will eventually come up against problems like this:

NATIVE SPEAKER: How long are you here for?
LEARNER: I am here since two weeks.
NATIVE SPEAKER: No, I mean, how long are you staying?
LEARNER: I am staying since two weeks.

Learners need to learn not only what forms are possible, but what particular forms will express their particular meanings. Seen from this perspective, grammar is a tool for making meaning. The implication for language teachers is that the learner's attention needs to be focused not only on the forms of the language, but on the meanings these forms convey.

Two kinds of meaning

But what meanings do these grammatical forms convey? There are at least two kinds of meaning and these reflect the two main purposes of language. The first is to represent the world as we experience it, and the second is to influence how things happen in the world, specifically in our relations with other people. These purposes are called, respectively, language's **representational** and its **interpersonal** functions.

In its representational role language reflects the way we perceive the world. For example, things happen in the world, and these events or processes are conveyed by (or **encoded** in) **verbs**:

> The sun **set**.

Many of these events and processes are initiated by people or things, which are typically encoded in nouns, and which in turn form the **subject** of the verb:

> **The children** are playing.

And these events and processes often have an effect on other things, also nouns: the thing or person affected is often the **object** of the verb:

> The dog chased **the cat**.

These events take place in particular circumstances – in some time or some place or in some way – and these circumstances are typically encoded in **adverbials**:

> The children are playing **in the garden**.
> The sun sets **at seven-thirty**.
> The dog chased the cat **playfully**.

Time can also be conveyed by the use of **tense**:

> The children **were** playing in the garden.
> The sun **set** at seven-thirty.

Finally, events and processes can be seen in their entirety:

> The sun set.

Or they can be seen as having stages, as unfolding in time:

> The sun was setting.

The difference between these last two examples is a difference of **aspect**. Tense and aspect can combine to form a wide range of meanings that, in English at least, are considered important:

> The sun is setting.
> The sun has set.
> The sun has been setting.
> The sun had set.
> etc.

The second main role of language – its interpersonal role – is typically reflected in the way we use grammar to ease the task of getting things done.

There is a difference, for example, between:

Tickets!
Tickets, please.
Can you show me your tickets?
May I see your tickets?
Would you mind if I had a look at your tickets?

Please is one way – a lexical way – for softening the force of a command. A similar effect can be achieved by using **modal verbs** such as *can*, *may* and *might*. **Modality**, then, is a grammatical means by which interpersonal meaning can be conveyed.

These grammatical categories – subjects, objects, verbs, adverbials, tense, aspect and modality – are just some of the ways in which grammar is used to fine-tune the meanings we wish to express, and for which words on their own are barely adequate. It follows that in learning a new language learners need to see how the forms of the language match the range of meanings – both representational and interpersonal – that they need to express and understand.

Grammar and function

So far, we have talked about meaning as if the meaning of a sentence was simply a case of unpacking its words and its grammar. But look at this exchange (from the film *Clueless*) between a father and the young man who has come to take his daughter out:

FATHER: Do you drink?
YOUNG MAN: No, thanks, I'm cool.
FATHER: I'm not offering, I'm asking IF you drink. Do you think I'd
             offer alcohol to teenage drivers taking my daughter out?

Why did the young man misunderstand the father's question, misconstruing a request for information as an offer? Was it the words he didn't understand? Or the grammar? Or both? Clearly not. What he misunderstood was the father's intended meaning. He misunderstood the **function** of the question.

There is more than one meaning to the question *Do you drink?* There is the literal meaning – something like *Are you a drinker of alcohol?* And there is the meaning that the question can have in certain contexts – that of an offer of a drink. When we process language we are not only trying to make sense of the words and the grammar; we are also trying to infer the speaker's (or writer's) intention, or, to put it another way, the **function** of what they are saying or writing.

In the mid-seventies the relation between grammar and function became an important issue for teachers. Writers of language teaching materials attempted to move the emphasis away from the learning of grammatical structures independent of their use, and on to learning how to function in a language, how to communicate. It would be useful, it was argued, to match forms with their functions.

Certain form-function matches are fairly easily identifiable. For example, the form *Would you like ... ?* is typically used to function as an invitation or offer. The form *If only I hadn't* ... commonly initiates the expression of a regret. Less clear cut is the way that the function of *warning*, for example, is expressed, as the following examples demonstrate:

You'd better not do that.
I wouldn't do that, if I were you.
Mind you don't do that.
If you do that, you'll be in trouble.
Do that and you'll be in trouble.

This shows that one function can be expressed by several different forms. In the same way, one form can express a variety of functions. For example, the form *If* ..., ... *will* ... can express a wide range of functions:

If you do that, you'll be in trouble. (warning)
If you lie down, you'll feel better. (advice)
If it rains, we'll take a taxi. (plan)
If you pass your driving test, I'll buy you a car. (promise)
etc.

Despite this lack of a one-to-one match between form and function, materials writers have felt it useful to organise at least some grammatical structures under functional labels, such as *Inviting*, *Making plans*, *Requesting things*, *Making comparisons* etc.

There are conventional ways of doing things with language, such as making requests. But this still doesn't help solve the problem of knowing when *Do you drink?* means *Would you like a drink?* or something else. In the end, in order to successfully match form and function it is necessary to be able to read clues from the context to understand the speaker's meaning. Teaching grammar out of context is likely to lead to similar misunderstandings as in the example from *Clueless*, a point that will be taken up in Chapter 5.

Spoken grammar and written grammar

A: Great sausages, these, aren't they?
B: Yes. The ingredients are guaranteed free of additives and artificial colouring.
A: Had to laugh, though. The bloke that makes them, he was telling me, he doesn't eat them himself. Want a ciggie?
B: No, thanks. Patrons are requested to refrain from smoking while other guests are dining ...

It should be obvious that there is a clash of two styles of English here: while speaker A's talk seems to display language features appropriate to casual conversation among friends, speaker B's contributions are more typical of formal written language. Thus, speaker A's vocabulary choices are characteristic of speech, e.g. *great*, *bloke*, *a ciggie*, while speaker B's are more commonly found in writing: *grateful*, *requested*, *refrain*. These differences extend to grammar, too. Speaker A omits words ([*I*] *had to laugh*), uses question tags (*aren't they?*), and has sentences with two subjects: *The bloke that makes them, he ...* These are common features of **spoken grammar**.

Speaker B, on the other hand, uses more syntactically complex constructions such as passive structures (*The ingredients are guaranteed ...*, *Patrons are requested ...*) and subordinate clauses (*... while other guests are dining*). These are features associated more with **written grammar**.

Until recently, the grammar presented to learners of English has been based entirely on written grammar. This accounts for the often stilted style of many traditional coursebook dialogues. It is only recently that spoken grammar has been closely studied and that arguments have been advanced in favour of teaching it. One problem with this shift of focus is that spoken English often has strong regional and idiomatic features. These may be difficult for the learner to understand, and also inappropriate for use in the kinds of contexts in which many learners will be operating. Most learners of English as a foreign language will be using English to communicate with other non-native speakers. For the purposes of mutual intelligibility the best model of English for this type of learner may be a kind of neutral English without marked regional or cultural features, or without a strong bias to either the spoken or written mode.

Grammar syllabuses

For most practising teachers the decision as to what to teach, and in what order, has largely been made for them by their coursebook. Even if not working from a coursebook, most teachers are expected to work to a programme of some sort, the most common form of which is a list of grammar items. It might pay to be familiar with the principles on which such syllabuses are based.

A **syllabus** is to teaching what an itinerary is to package tourism. It is a pre-planned, itemised, account of the route: it tells the teacher (and the students, if they have access to it) what is to be covered and in what order. It is informed by two sets of decisions:

- selection – that is, what is to be included?
- grading – that is, in what order are the selected items to be dealt with?

The criteria for selecting which items to put in a syllabus are essentially two:

- usefulness
- frequency

Note that it is not always the case that the most frequently occurring items are the most useful. The ten most frequent words in English are *the, of, and, to, a, in, that, I, it* and *was*. Together they constitute nearly one-fifth of all English text. But you would be hard-pressed to make a sentence out of them, let alone have a conversation. And, while lexical frequency is relatively easy to calculate, working out the frequency of grammatical structures is more difficult. As computer databases become more sophisticated, frequency information is likely to improve. Meanwhile, syllabus designers still tend to operate by hunch.

Finally, questions of usefulness will be dependent on the specific needs of the learner. For example, if a group of learners need English mainly in order to write in English they will need to attend to features of written grammar such as passives, subordination, and reported speech etc. If, on the other hand, they mainly need to be able to speak, those features will be less useful. Nevertheless, it is fair to hypothesise a **core grammar** that will be useful to all learners, whatever their needs.

Here, for example, is a checklist of items (in alphabetical order) that are shared by four current beginners' courses:

articles: *a/an, the*
adjectives: comparatives and superlatives
be: present and past
can/can't: ability
can/can't: requests
going to: future
have got: possession
like + noun
like + *-ing*
past simple
possessive adjectives (*my, your, our* etc.)
prepositions of place and time
present continuous
present simple
should (advice)
would (offers)
will (future)

Criteria for **grading** the syllabus – that is, for putting the selected items in order – include:

- complexity
- learnability
- teachability

An item is **complex** if it has a number of elements: the more elements, the more complex it is. For example, a structure such as the present perfect continuous (*She has been reading*) is more complex than the present continuous (*She is reading*), while the future perfect continuous is more complex still (*She will have been reading*). Logic suggests that the less complex structures should be taught before the more complex ones.

In terms of the number of operations involved, question forms in English can be relatively simple. Take for example, this transformation:

Chris is English → Is Chris English?

The operation here is a simple one: to form the question simply invert the subject (*Chris*) and the verb (*is*). However, to form the question for *Chris speaks English* a further operation is required before subject–verb inversion can take place:

Chris speaks English → Chris [does] speak English
Chris [does] speak English → Does Chris speak English?

Taking a purely mechanical view of language, it would again seem logical to teach simple, one-step operations before more complex ones.

The **learnability** of an item was traditionally measured by its complexity: the more simple, the more learnable. However, traditional notions of learnability have been called into question recently, in the light of research into what is called the **natural order** of language acquisition. While this research is still far from conclusive, it seems that all learners acquire grammatical items in a fairly predictable order, and this happens irrespective of either their mother tongue or the order in which they are actually taught these structures. Most students will go through a stage of saying *it going* for example, before they graduate to *it's going*, even though they may have a similar structure in their mother tongue. Similarly, learners tend to pick up irregular past forms (*went*, *saw*, *bought* etc.) before regular ones (*worked*, *lived*, *started* etc.), while the third person *-s* ending (*she swims*, *Ed works*) is picked up later still. The question is, should these 'natural order' findings affect the design of grammar syllabuses?

First of all, we need to make a distinction between what learners are exposed to (**input**) and what they are expected to produce (**output**). The 'natural order' research provides evidence of the order of output only. Even if we accept that the accurate production of grammatical structures seems to follow a pre-determined route, this does not mean that learners should be exposed to only those structures and in only that order. Evidence suggests that classroom learners need a varied diet of language input. It may be that the findings of the natural order research have less to do with syllabus design than with teacher attitude. These findings suggest that, since some grammar items take longer to learn than others, teachers need not insist on immediate accuracy.

A third factor that might influence the selection and ordering of items on a grammatical syllabus is an item's **teachability**. The fact that it is easy to demonstrate the meaning of the present continuous (*I am walking*, *she is writing* etc.) has meant that it is often included early in beginners' syllabuses, despite the fact that it has a relatively low frequency of occurrence compared, say, to the present simple (*I walk*, *she writes*). The rules for the use of articles (*a*, *the*) on the other hand, are difficult either to describe or to demonstrate. So, despite being among the most frequently used words in the language, their formal presentation is usually delayed until a relatively advanced level.

Finally, it is worth pointing out that not all syllabuses are, or have been, designed on a grammatical basis. With the advent of the communicative approach in the mid-1970s there was a reaction away from purely form-based syllabuses to syllabuses that were organised according to categories of **meaning**. For example, **functional** syllabuses, as we have seen, were organised around the communicative purposes for which language is used, such as: *asking directions*, *describing things*, *inviting* etc.

Other organising principles for a syllabus include **tasks** (to design a video game and describe it; to write a poem and read it aloud etc.) **topics** (the home, travel, the environment, news etc.) and **genres** (office memos, informal letters, business presentations, casual conversation etc). Many courses nowadays attempt to accommodate the multi-layered nature of language by adopting multi-layered syllabuses. That is, they specify not only the grammar areas to be taught, but include functional and topical areas as well.

Grammar rules

In the *Longman Active Study Dictionary* 'rule' is defined as:

* a principle or order which guides behaviour, says how things are to be done etc, or
* the usual way that something happens.

With regard to grammar, the first type of rule is often called a **prescriptive** rule and the second a **descriptive** rule. For many people, grammar instruction is traditionally associated with the teaching of the first type of rules – that is, prescriptions as to what should be said (or written):

> Do not use *different to* and never use *different than*. Always use *different from*.

> Never use the passive when you can use the active.

> Use *shall* for the first person and *will* for second and third persons.

Second and foreign language teaching, on the other hand, is primarily concerned with descriptive rules, that is, with generalisations about what speakers of the language actually *do* say rather than with what they *should do*. Thus:

> You do not normally use *the* with proper nouns referring to people.
> (from *The COBUILD Student's Grammar of English*)

> We use *used to* with the infinitive (*used to do/used to smoke* etc.) to say that something regularly happened in the past but no longer happens.
> (from *English Grammar in Use* by Raymond Murphy)

Until recently most so-called descriptive rules were based on hunches and intuitions. There is much greater authority in descriptions of language since the advent of large computer databases of naturally occurring language, known as **corpora**. The following rule, for example, represents the traditional wisdom with regard to *some* and *any*:

1 As a general rule, use *some* in affirmative sentences, use *any* in questions and negative statements.
(from *English Structure Practice* by Gordon Drummond)

Statistical evidence provided by corpora has indicated that this rule oversimplifies the issue and that the following qualification needs to be made:

2 *Any* can mean 'it doesn't matter which'. With this meaning, *any* is common in affirmative sentences.
(from *How English Works* by Michael Swan and Catherine Walter)

This brings us to a further distinction that needs to be made with regard to descriptive rules. Compare, for example, rule 1 with the following:

3 The primary difference between *some* and *any* ... is that *some* is specific, though unspecified, while *any* is nonspecific. That is, *some* implies an amount or number that is known to the speaker. This difference tends to correlate with the difference between positive and negative contexts.
(from *A Comprehensive Grammar of the English Language* by Quirk et al.)

Rule 3 may be the truth, the whole truth, and nothing but the truth, but most learners of English (and many teachers) would find such concepts as *specific*, *nonspecific*, and *unspecified* difficult to untangle. Rule 1, on the other hand, makes up in simplicity for what it lacks in truth. It is accessible to learners and, as a rule of thumb, it will probably serve quite well until such time as the learner is ready to tackle a more truthful rule, such as rule 2. We need, therefore, to define a third category of rule: **pedagogic rules** – rules that make sense to learners while at the same time providing them with the means and confidence to generate language with a reasonable chance of success. Inevitably, such confidence is often achieved at the expense of the full picture. Teachers must, in the end, cater for the learner's needs rather than those of the grammarian.

With regard to pedagogic rules, a further distinction may be made between **rules of form** and **rules of use**. The following is a rule of form:

To form the past simple of regular verbs, add *-ed* to the infinitive
(from *A Practical English Grammar* by Thomson and Martinet)

This, on the other hand, is a rule of use:

The simple past tense is used to indicate past actions or states.
(from *English Structure Practice* by Gordon Drummond)

Rules of form are generally easier to formulate and are less controversial than rules of use. It is relatively easy to explain exceptions, such as *carried*, *loved*, *stopped* to the above rule of form for the past simple and to construct fairly watertight sub-rules that will handle them. But the following exceptions to the rule of use are less easily accommodated into a general rule about the past simple:

How did you say you *spelt* your name?
I was wondering if you *had* any detective novels.
It's time they *went* to bed.

Rules of use, being heavily dependent on contextual factors, are seldom captured in terms that are black or white. The slippery nature of rules of use can be a cause of frustration for both learners and teachers alike, and is one argument that supports the teaching of language through examples (see Chapter 4) or by means of contexts (see Chapter 5).

Conclusions   In this chapter we have defined grammar as:
- a description of the rules for forming sentences, including an account of the meanings that these forms convey

and said that:
- grammar adds meanings that are not easily inferable from the immediate context.

The kinds of meanings realised by grammar are principally:
- representational – that is, grammar enables us to use language to describe the world in terms of how, when and where things happen, and
- interpersonal – that is, grammar facilitates the way we interact with other people when, for example, we need to get things done using language.

With regard to the relationship between form and meaning, we have seen that:
- there is no one-to-one match between grammatical form and communicative function, and that
- contextual information plays a key role in our interpretation of what a speaker means.

We have also seen that:
- while traditional grammar is based on the written form of the language, spoken language has its own distinctive grammar.

From the teaching point of view, we have looked at:
- ways that grammar can be organised into a teaching syllabus according to such criteria as complexity, learnability, and teachability
- ways that grammar rules can be formulated, according to whether they are prescriptive, descriptive or pedagogic, and whether they focus on form or on use.

Looking ahead   We have looked briefly at what grammar is, what it does, and how it can be organised and described. We now need to address the role of grammar in language learning. By discussing grammar syllabuses we have implied that grammar has a role, perhaps a central one, in teaching. But what justification is there for such a view?

In the next chapter we explore the arguments for and against the teaching of grammar.

2 Why teach grammar?

- **Attitudes to grammar**
- **The case for grammar**
- **The case against grammar**
- **Grammar and methods**
- **Grammar now**
- **Basic principles for grammar teaching**

Attitudes to grammar

In 1622 a certain Joseph Webbe, schoolmaster and textbook writer, wrote: 'No man can run speedily to the mark of language that is shackled ... with grammar precepts.' He maintained that grammar could be picked up through simply communicating: 'By exercise of reading, writing, and speaking ... all things belonging to Grammar, will without labour, and whether we will or no, thrust themselves upon us.'

Webbe was one of the earliest educators to question the value of grammar instruction, but certainly not the last. In fact, no other issue has so preoccupied theorists and practitioners as the grammar debate, and the history of language teaching is essentially the history of the claims and counterclaims for and against the teaching of grammar. Differences in attitude to the role of grammar underpin differences between methods, between teachers, and between learners. It is a subject that everyone involved in language teaching and learning has an opinion on. And these opinions are often strongly and uncompromisingly stated. Here, for example, are a number of recent statements on the subject:

'There is no doubt that a knowledge – implicit or explicit – of grammatical rules is essential for the mastery of a language.'
(Penny Ur, a teacher trainer, and author of *Grammar Practice Activities*)

'The effects of grammar teaching ... appear to be peripheral and fragile.'
(Stephen Krashen, an influential, if controversial, applied linguist)

'A sound knowledge of grammar is essential if pupils are going to use English creatively.'
(Tom Hutchinson, a coursebook writer)

'Grammar is not very important: The majority of languages have a very complex grammar. English has little grammar and consequently it is not very important to understand it.'
(From the publicity of a London language school)

'Grammar is not the basis of language acquisition, and the balance of linguistic research clearly invalidates any view to the contrary.'
(Michael Lewis, a popular writer on teaching methods)

Since so little is known (still!) about how languages are acquired, this book will try to avoid taking an entrenched position on the issue. Rather, by sifting the arguments for and against, it is hoped that readers will be in a better position to make up their own minds. Let's first look at the case for grammar.

The case for grammar

There are many arguments for putting grammar in the foreground in second language teaching. Here are seven of them:

The sentence-machine argument

Part of the process of language learning must be what is sometimes called **item-learning** – that is the memorisation of individual items such as words and phrases. However, there is a limit to the number of items a person can both retain and retrieve. Even travellers' phrase books have limited usefulness – good for a three-week holiday, but there comes a point where we need to learn some patterns or rules to enable us to generate new sentences. That is to say, grammar. Grammar, after all, is a description of the regularities in a language, and knowledge of these regularities provides the learner with the means to generate a potentially enormous number of original sentences. The number of possible new sentences is constrained only by the vocabulary at the learner's command and his or her creativity. Grammar is a kind of '**sentence-making machine**'. It follows that the teaching of grammar offers the learner the means for potentially limitless linguistic creativity.

The fine-tuning argument

As we saw in Chapter 1, the purpose of grammar seems to be to allow for greater subtlety of meaning than a merely lexical system can cater for. While it is possible to get a lot of communicative mileage out of simply stringing words and phrases together, there comes a point where 'Me Tarzan, you Jane'-type language fails to deliver, both in terms of intelligibility and in terms of appropriacy. This is particularly the case for written language, which generally needs to be more explicit than spoken language. For example, the following errors are likely to confuse the reader:

Last Monday night I was boring in my house.

After speaking a lot time with him I thought that him attracted me.

We took a wrong plane and when I saw it was very later because the plane took up.

Five years ago I would want to go to India but in that time anybody of my friends didn't want to go.

The teaching of grammar, it is argued, serves as a corrective against the kind of ambiguity represented in these examples.

The fossilisation argument

It is possible for highly motivated learners with a particular aptitude for languages to achieve amazing levels of proficiency without any formal study. But more often 'pick it up as you go along' learners reach a language plateau beyond which it is very difficult to progress. To put it technically, their linguistic competence **fossilises**. Research suggests that learners who receive no instruction seem to be at risk of fossilising sooner than those who do receive instruction. Of course, this doesn't necessarily mean taking formal lessons – the grammar study can be self-directed, as in this case (from Christopher Isherwood's autobiographical novel *Christopher and his Kind*):

> Humphrey said suddenly, 'You speak German so well – tell me, why don't you ever use the subjunctive mood?' Christopher had to admit that he didn't know how to. In the days when he had studied German, he had left the subjunctive to be dealt with later, since it wasn't absolutely essential and he was in a hurry. By this time he could hop through the language without its aid, like an agile man with only one leg. But now Christopher set himself to master the subjunctive. Very soon, he had done so. Proud of this accomplishment, he began showing off whenever he talked: 'had it not been for him, I should never have asked myself what I would do if they were to ... etc, etc.' Humphrey was much amused.

The advance-organiser argument

Grammar instruction might also have a delayed effect. The researcher Richard Schmidt kept a diary of his experience learning Portuguese in Brazil. Initially he had enrolled in formal language classes where there was a heavy emphasis on grammar. When he subsequently left these classes to travel in Brazil his Portuguese made good progress, a fact he attributed to the use he was making of it. However, as he interacted naturally with Brazilians he was aware that certain features of the talk – certain grammatical items – seemed to catch his attention. He **noticed** them. It so happened that these items were also items he had studied in his classes. What's more, being more noticeable, these items seemed to stick. Schmidt concluded that **noticing** is a prerequisite for acquisition. The grammar teaching he had received previously, while insufficient in itself to turn him into a fluent Portuguese speaker, had primed him to notice what might otherwise have gone unnoticed, and hence had indirectly influenced his learning. It had acted as a kind of **advance organiser** for his later acquisition of the language.

The discrete item argument

Language – any language – seen from 'outside', can seem to be a gigantic, shapeless mass, presenting an insuperable challenge for the learner. Because grammar consists of an apparently finite set of rules, it can help to reduce the apparent enormity of the language learning task for both teachers and students. By tidying language up and organising it into neat categories (sometimes called **discrete items**), grammarians make language digestible.

A discrete item is any unit of the grammar system that is sufficiently narrowly defined to form the focus of a lesson or an exercise: e.g. *the present continuous*, *the definite article*, *possessive pronouns*. *Verbs*, on the other hand, or *sentences* are not categories that are sufficiently discrete for teaching purposes, since they allow for further sub-categories. Each discrete item can be isolated from the language that normally envelops it. It can then be slotted into a syllabus of other discrete items, and targeted for individual attention and testing. Other ways of packaging language for teaching purposes are less easily organised into a syllabus. For example, communicative functions, such as *asking favours*, *making requests*, *expressing regrets*, and text type categories, such as *narratives*, *instructions*, *phone conversations*, are often thought to be too large and unruly for the purposes of lesson design.

The rule-of-law argument
It follows from the discrete-item argument that, since grammar is a system of learnable rules, it lends itself to a view of teaching and learning known as **transmission**. A transmission view sees the role of education as the transfer of a body of knowledge (typically in the form of facts and rules) from those that have the knowledge to those that do not. Such a view is typically associated with the kind of institutionalised learning where rules, order, and discipline are highly valued. The need for rules, order and discipline is particularly acute in large classes of unruly and unmotivated teenagers – a situation that many teachers of English are confronted with daily. In this sort of situation grammar offers the teacher a structured system that can be taught and tested in methodical steps. The alternative – allowing learners simply to experience the language through communication – may simply be out of the question.

The learner expectations argument (1)
Regardless of the theoretical and ideological arguments for or against grammar teaching, many learners come to language classes with fairly fixed expectations as to what they will do there. These expectations may derive from previous classroom experience of language learning. They may also derive from experience of classrooms in general where (traditionally, at least) teaching is of the transmission kind mentioned above. On the other hand, their expectations that teaching will be grammar-focused may stem from frustration experienced at trying to pick up a second language in a non-classroom setting, such as through self-study, or through immersion in the target language culture. Such students may have enrolled in language classes specifically to ensure that the learning experience is made more efficient and systematic. The teacher who ignores this expectation by encouraging learners simply to experience language is likely to frustrate and alienate them.

The case against grammar

Just as arguments have been marshalled in favour of grammar teaching, likewise several cases have been made against it. Here are the main ones:

The knowledge-how argument

I know what is involved in riding a bike: keeping your balance, pedalling, steering by means of the handlebars and so on. This does not mean to say that I know how to ride a bike. The same analogy applies to language learning. It can be viewed as a body of knowledge – such as vocabulary and grammar. Or it can be viewed as a skill (or a complex set of skills). If you take the language-is-skill point of view, then it follows that, like bike riding, you learn it by doing it, not by studying it. Learning-by-doing is what is called **experiential** learning. Much of the bad press associated with intellectual approaches to language learning – through the learning of copious grammar rules, for example – stems from the failure on the part of the learner to translate rules into skills. It is a failure that accounts for this observation by Jerome K. Jerome, writing in *Three Men on the Bummel* about a typical English schoolboy's French:

> He may be able to tell the time, or make a few guarded observations concerning the weather. No doubt he could repeat a goodly number of irregular verbs by heart ... [But] when the proud parent takes his son to Dieppe merely to discover that the lad does not know enough to call a cab, he abuses not the system but the innocent victim.

Proponents of the 'knowledge-how' view might argue that what the boy needed was not so much grammar as classroom experience that simulated the kind of conditions in which he would eventually use his French.

The communication argument

There is more to knowing a language than knowing its grammar. It is one thing to know that *Do you drink?* is a present simple question. It is another thing to know that it can function as an offer. This simple observation is at the heart of what is now called the **Communicative Approach**, or **Communicative Language Teaching** (CLT). From the 1970s on, theorists have been arguing that grammatical knowledge (linguistic competence) is merely one component of what they call **communicative competence**. Communicative competence involves knowing how to use the grammar and vocabulary of the language to achieve communicative goals, and knowing how to do this in a socially appropriate way.

Two schools of thought emerged as to the best means of achieving the objectives of this communicative approach. Both schools placed a high premium on putting the language to communicative use. But they differed as to when you should do this. The first – or shallow-end approach – might be summed up as the view that you learn a language in order to use it. That is: learn the rules and then apply them in life-like communication. The more radical line, however, is that you use a language in order to learn it. Proponents of this deep-end approach take an experiential view of learning: you learn to communicate by communicating. They argue that, by means of activities that engage the learner in life-like communication, the grammar will be acquired virtually unconsciously. Studying the rules of grammar is simply a waste of valuable time.

The acquisition argument

The fact that we all learned our first language without being taught grammar rules has not escaped theorists. If it works for the first, why shouldn't it work for the second? This is an argument that has been around at least since Joseph Webbe's day (see page 14). It received a new impetus in the 1970s through the work of the applied linguist Stephen Krashen. Krashen makes the distinction between *learning*, on the one hand, and *acquisition*, on the other. Learning, according to Krashen, results from formal instruction, typically in grammar, and is of limited use for real communication. Acquisition, however, is a natural process: it is the process by which the first language is picked up, and by which other languages are picked up solely through contact with speakers of those languages. Acquisition occurs (according to Krashen) when the learner is exposed to the right input in a stress-free environment so that innate learning capacities are triggered. Success in a second language is due to acquisition, not learning, he argues. Moreover, he claims that learnt knowledge can never become acquired knowledge.

Krashen's theory had an important influence on language teaching practices, especially with teachers who were disenchanted with the 'drill-and-repeat' type methodology that prevailed in the 1950s and 1960s. Rejection of the formal study of grammar is central to Krashen's 'Natural Approach'.

The natural order argument

Krashen's acquisition/learning hypothesis drew heavily on studies that suggest there is a natural order of acquisition of grammatical items, irrespective of the order in which they are taught (see page 10). This view derives partly from the work of the linguist Noam Chomsky. Chomsky argues that humans are 'hard-wired' to learn languages: that is, there are universal principles of grammar that we are born with. The idea of an innate **universal grammar** helps explain similarities in the developmental order in first language acquisition as well as in second language acquisition. It explains why English children, Thai teenagers and Saudi adults all go through a *I no like fish* stage before progressing to *I don't like fish*. It also suggests that attempts to subvert the natural order by sticking rigidly to a traditional grammar syllabus and insisting on immediate accuracy are foredoomed. In short, the natural order argument insists that a textbook grammar is not, nor can ever become, a mental grammar.

The lexical chunks argument

We have already noted the fact that language learning seems to involve an element of item-learning. Vocabulary learning is largely **item-learning**. So too is the retention of whole phrases, idioms, social formulae etc. in the form of what are sometimes called **chunks** of language. Chunks are larger than words but often less than sentences. Here are some common examples:

excuse me?
so far so good
what on earth?
have a nice day
be that as it may
if you ask me
not on your life
here you are

Acquiring chunks of language not only saves the learner planning time in the cut-and-thrust of real interaction, but seems to play a role in language development too. It has been argued that many of the expressions that young children pick up, like *all-gone*, or *gimme* (as in *gimme the ball*), are learned as chunks and only later unpacked into their component parts. Once unpacked, new combinations, such as *give her the ball* start to emerge. It has been argued that this process of analysing previously stored chunks plays an important role in first language acquisition.

How much of second language acquisition involves item-learning as opposed to rule-learning is still an open question. Nevertheless, in recent years there has been a growing recognition of the importance of word- and chunk-learning, such that some writers have proposed a **lexical approach** to teaching, in contrast to the traditional emphasis on sentence grammar. Among other things, a lexical approach promotes the learning of frequently used and fairly formulaic expressions (*Have you ever been … ? Would you like a … ?*) rather than the study of rather abstract grammatical categories such as the present perfect or conditionals.

The learner expectations argument (2)

While many learners come to language classes in the expectation that at least some of the time they will be studying the grammar of the language, there are many others who may already have had years of grammar study at school and are urgently in need of a chance to put this knowledge to work. Questionnaires of adult students in general English courses almost invariably identify 'conversation' as a high priority, and these statements (from *Looking at Language Classrooms*, Cambridge University Press) by a range of EFL students studying in Britain are typical:

> 'In Germany there's more homework, grammar exercises, and things like that. Here, I think you've got more chance to speak and therefore learn the language.'

> 'Sometimes, speaking and things like that help a lot, because if you don't speak English, and just do writing exercises, it's no good.'

> 'I like having conversations because, yes, grammar is important, but it's not much fun …'

The learner expectation argument cuts both ways: some learners demand grammar, others just want to talk. It's the teacher's job to respond sensitively to these expectations, to provide a balance where possible, and even to negotiate a compromise.

Before attempting to bring the grammar debate up to date, and to draw some conclusions from recent research evidence, it may pay to briefly sketch in the way attitudes to grammar teaching have influenced the ebb and flow of different teaching methods.

Grammar and methods

In the last century the architects of language teaching methods have been preoccupied with two basic design decisions concerning grammar:

- Should the method adhere to a grammar syllabus?
- Should the rules of grammar be made explicit?

The various ways they answered these questions help distinguish the different methods from each other. What follows is a potted history of methods in the light of their approach to these issues.

Grammar-Translation, as its name suggests, took grammar as the starting point for instruction. Grammar-Translation courses followed a grammar syllabus and lessons typically began with an explicit statement of the rule, followed by exercises involving translation into and out of the mother tongue.

The **Direct Method**, which emerged in the mid- to late-nineteenth century, challenged the way that Grammar-Translation focused exclusively on the written language. By claiming to be a 'natural' method, the Direct Method prioritised oral skills, and, while following a syllabus of grammar structures, rejected explicit grammar teaching. The learners, it was supposed, picked up the grammar in much the same way as children pick up the grammar of their mother tongue, simply by being immersed in language.

Audiolingualism, a largely North American invention, stayed faithful to the Direct Method belief in the primacy of speech, but was even more strict in its rejection of grammar teaching. Audiolingualism derived its theoretical base from behaviourist psychology, which considered language as simply a form of behaviour, to be learned through the formation of correct habits. Habit formation was a process in which the application of rules played no part. The Audiolingual syllabus consisted of a graded list of sentence patterns, which, although not necessarily labelled as such, were grammatical in origin. These patterns formed the basis of pattern-practice **drills**, the distinguishing feature of Audiolingual classroom practice.

Noam Chomsky's claim, in the late 1950s, that language ability is not habituated behaviour but an innate human capacity, prompted a reassessment of drill-and-repeat type teaching practices. The view that we are equipped at birth for language acquisition led, as we saw on page 19, to Krashen's belief that formal instruction was unnecessary. His **Natural Approach** does away with both a grammar syllabus and explicit rule-giving. Instead, learners are exposed to large doses of **comprehensible input**. Innate processes convert this input into output, in time. Like the Direct Method, the Natural Approach attempts to replicate the conditions of first language acquisition. Grammar, according to this scenario, is irrelevant.

The development, in the 1970s, of **Communicative Language Teaching** (CLT) was motivated by developments in the new science of socio-linguistics, and the belief that communicative competence consists of more than simply the knowledge of the rules of grammar (see above, page 18). Nevertheless, CLT, in its shallow-end version at least, did not reject grammar teaching out of hand. In fact, grammar was still the main component of the syllabus of CLT courses, even if it was dressed up in **functional** labels: *asking the way, talking about yourself, making future plans* etc. Explicit attention to grammar rules was not incompatible with communicative practice, either. Chomsky, after all, had claimed that language was rule-governed, and this seemed to suggest to theorists that explicit rule-giving may have a place after all. This belief was around at about the time that CLT was being developed, and was readily absorbed into it. Grammar rules reappeared in coursebooks, and grammar teaching re-emerged in classrooms, often, it must be said, at the expense of communicative practice.

Deep-end CLT, on the other hand, rejected both grammar-based syllabuses and grammar instruction. A leading proponent of this view was N.S. Prabhu, a teacher of English in southern India. In his **Bangalore Project**, he attempted to replicate natural acquisition processes by having students work through a syllabus of **tasks** for which no formal grammar instruction was supposedly needed nor provided. Successful completion of the task – for example, following a map – was the lesson objective, rather than successful application of a rule of grammar. The Bangalore Project was the predecessor of what is now known as **task-based learning**. Task-based learning has more recently relaxed its approach to grammar, largely through recognition of the value of a **focus on form** (see below, page 24).

To summarise the story so far: to the first of the questions posed above (*Should the method adhere to a grammatical syllabus?*) most approaches to language teaching up until the 1970s have answered firmly *Yes*. The actual form of the syllabus differed considerably from method to method, but, until such organising categories as **functions** or **tasks** were proposed, syllabuses were essentially grammar-based.

On the question of the explicitness of rule teaching there is a clear divide between those methods that seek to mirror the processes of first language acquisition – such as the Direct Method and the Natural Approach – and those – such as Grammar-Translation – that see second language acquisition as a more intellectual process. The former methods reject grammar instruction, while the latter accept a role for conscious rule-learning.

Finally, even in methods where rules are made explicit, there may be a different emphasis with regard to the way the learner arrives at these rules. In some approaches, such as Grammar-Translation, the rules are simply presented to the learner, who then goes on to apply them through the study and manipulation of examples (a **deductive** approach: see Chapter 3). Other approaches, including the shallow-end form of the communicative approach, often require the learners first to study examples and work the rules out for themselves (an **inductive** approach: see Chapter 4).

At the risk of over-simplifying matters, the following chart indicates the relative importance these methods attach to the teaching of grammar:

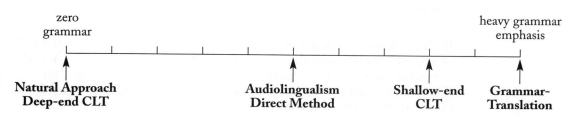

zero grammar · · · · · · · · · · heavy grammar emphasis

**Natural Approach
Deep-end CLT** · **Audiolingualism
Direct Method** · **Shallow-end
CLT** · **Grammar-
Translation**

Grammar now

What, then, is the status of grammar now? What is common practice with regard to the teaching of grammar, and what directions for future practice are suggested by recent and current research?

Firstly, it is important to establish the fact that 'grammar teaching' can mean different things to different people. It may mean simply teaching to a grammar syllabus but otherwise not making any reference to grammar in the classroom at all (as was the case with Audiolingualism). On the other hand it may mean teaching to a communicative syllabus (e.g. of functions or of tasks) but dealing with grammar questions that arise in the course of doing communicative activities. This is sometimes called **covert** grammar teaching. More typically, grammar teaching means teaching to a grammar syllabus and explicitly presenting the rules of grammar, using grammar terminology. This is known as **overt** grammar teaching.

Lately, a good deal has been written about a grammar revival. There is a widespread belief that, with the introduction of Communicative Language Teaching, attention to grammar was eclipsed by an emphasis on experiential learning and purely communicative goals. This is only partly true: syllabuses did appear in the 1970s that appeared to marginalise grammar in favour of functions. But, as was pointed out in the previous section, a closer look at these syllabuses shows that they often had a strong grammar basis. And a glance at so-called communicative coursebooks confirms that grammar explanations are much more conspicuous now than they were, say, in the heyday of either the Direct Method or Audiolingualism.

The view that CLT deposed grammar may also stem from a tendency to equate grammar with **accuracy**. It is true that, in comparison with Audiolingualism, CLT has tended to place more weight on being intelligible than on being correct. Such an emphasis need not be at the expense of attention to the rules of grammar, however. Relaxing on accuracy simply acknowledges the fact that the rules of grammar take a long time to establish themselves, and that, in the meantime, the learners' wish to communicate should not be needlessly frustrated.

It is also true that the deep-end version of CLT, as promoted by Prabhu (see page 22), was hostile to explicit grammar teaching. But this was relatively short-lived, and, while of enormous interest from a theoretical perspective, it seems to have had little or no influence on global classroom practice. If grammar ever went away, it was only very briefly and not very far.

The sense that we are experiencing a grammar revival has been underlined by the emergence of two influential theoretical concepts:

- focus on form
- consciousness-raising

Both concepts owe something to the work of Stephen Krashen, even if only as a reaction to his claim that classroom teaching is a waste of time. You will remember that Krashen distinguishes between acquisition and learning. Grammar teaching – that is, attention to the forms of the language – lies in the domain of learning and, says Krashen, has little or no influence on language acquisition. More recently, research suggests that without some attention to **form**, learners run the risk of **fossilisation**. A **focus on form** does not necessarily mean a return to drill-and-repeat type methods of teaching. Nor does it mean the use of an off-the-shelf grammar syllabus. A focus on form may simply mean correcting a mistake. In this sense, a focus on form is compatible with a task-based approach.

Related to the notion of focus on form is the notion of **consciousness-raising**. Krashen argued that acquisition is a largely unconscious process. All that is needed to trigger it are large doses of comprehensible input. Other theorists have argued that the learner's role is perhaps less passive than Krashen implies, and that acquisition involves conscious processes, of which the most fundamental is **attention**. We have seen how Schmidt (see page 16) concluded that **noticing** spoken language items in Brazil helped his Portuguese. It follows that helping learners attend to language items may help them acquire them. Pointing out features of the grammatical system is thus a form of consciousness-raising. It may not lead directly and instantly to the acquisition of the item in question. But it may nevertheless trigger a train of mental processes that in time will result in accurate and appropriate production.

It might seem that we have come full circle, and that grammar consciousness-raising is simply a smart term for what was once called grammar **presentation**. But presentation is usually paired with **practice**, implying immediate – and accurate – output. Consciousness-raising, on the other hand, does not necessarily entail production: it may simply exist at the level of understanding. And remembering. In fact, put simply, that's what raised consciousness is: the state of remembering, having understood something.

To sum up: if the teacher uses techniques that direct the learner's attention to form, and if the teacher provides activities that promote awareness of grammar, learning seems to result. We need, therefore, to add to the pro-grammar position the arguments for a **focus on form** and for **consciousness-raising**. Together they comprise the **paying-attention-to-form argument**. That is to say, learning seems to be enhanced when the learner's attention is directed to getting the forms right, and when the learner's attention is directed to features of the grammatical system.

These would seem to tip the balance in favour of grammar. While the 'anti-grammar' position is strongly and even fiercely argued, it tends to depend on one basic assumption, that is, that the processes of second language acquisition mirror those of first language acquisition. This is an assumption that is hotly debated. While there are certainly cases of adult learners who have reached near-native levels of proficiency in a second language simply through immersion in the second language culture, these tend to be exceptions rather than the rule. On the other hand, there are compelling arguments to support the view that without attention to form, including grammatical form, the learner is unlikely to progress beyond the most basic level of communication.

But this doesn't mean that grammar should be the goal of teaching, nor that a focus on form alone is sufficient. The goal of the communicative movement – communicative competence – embraces more than just grammar, and implies a focus on **meaning** as well. It may be that communicative competence is best achieved through communicating, through making meanings, and that grammar is a way of tidying these meanings up. If so, the teacher's energies should be directed mainly at providing opportunities for authentic language use, employing grammar as a resource rather than as an end in itself. As Leibniz is supposed to have said: 'A language is acquired through practice; it is merely perfected through grammar.'

Basic principles for grammar teaching

We have looked at the arguments for and against incorporating grammar into language teaching, and concluded that, on balance, there is a convincing case for a role for grammar. The remainder of the book will explore how this role can be realised in the classroom. It will be useful at this stage to draw up some basic rules of thumb for grammar teaching – rules of thumb which will serve as the criteria for evaluating the practical approaches that follow.

The E-Factor: Efficiency = economy, ease, and efficacy

Given that dealing with grammar is only a part of a teacher's activities, and given that classroom time is very limited, it would seem imperative that whatever grammar teaching is done is done as **efficiently** as possible. If, as has been suggested, the teacher's energies should be at least partly directed at getting learners to communicate, prolonged attention to grammar is difficult to justify. Likewise, if a grammar activity requires a great deal of time to set up or a lot of materials, is it the most efficient deployment of the teacher's limited time, energy and resources? When considering an activity for the presentation or practice of grammar the first question to ask, is: *How efficient is it?* Efficiency, in turn, can be broken down into three factors: **economy, ease**, and **efficacy**.

When presenting grammar, a sound rule of thumb is: the shorter the better. It has been shown that **economy** is a key factor in the training of technical skills: when learning how to drive a car or operate a computer, a little prior teaching seems to be more effective than a lot. The more the instructor piles on instructions, the more confused the trainee is likely to become. The same would seem to apply in language teaching: be economical.

Be economical, too, in terms of planning and resources. The **ease** factor recognises the fact that most teachers lead busy lives, have many classes, and simply cannot afford to sacrifice valuable free time preparing elaborate classroom materials. Of course, the investment of time and energy in the preparation of materials is often accompanied by a commitment on the part of the teacher to making them work. But, realistically, painstaking preparation is not always going to be possible. Generally speaking, the easier an activity is to set up, the better it is.

Finally, and most importantly: will it work? That is to say, what is its **efficacy**? This factor is the least easy to evaluate. We have to operate more on hunch than on hard data. Learning, like language, resists measurement. Of course, there are tests, and these can provide feedback to the teacher on the efficacy of the teaching/learning process. Nevertheless, testing is notoriously problematic (see Chapter 9 for a discussion on this). Moreover, there is much greater scepticism nowadays as to the extent that teaching causes learning. This need not undermine our faith in the classroom as a good place for language learning. We now know a lot more about what constitute the best conditions for learning. If teachers can't directly cause learning, they can at least provide the optimal conditions for it.

As we have seen (page 24), a prerequisite for learning is **attention**. So the efficacy of a grammar activity can be partly measured by the degree of attention it arouses. This means trying to exclude from the focus of the learner's attention any distracting or irrelevant details. Attention without **understanding**, however, is probably a waste of time, so efficacy will in part depend on the amount and quality of contextual information, explanation and checking. Finally, understanding without **memory** would seem to be equally ineffective, and so the efficacy of a presentation will also depend on how memorable it is.

None of these conditions, however, will be sufficient if there is a lack of **motivation** and, in the absence of some external motivational factor (for example, an examination, or the anticipation of opportunities to use the language), it is the teacher's job to choose tasks and materials that engage the learners. Tasks and materials that are involving, that are relevant to their needs, that have an achievable outcome, and that have an element of challenge while providing the necessary support, are more likely to be motivating than those that do not have these qualities.

Efficiency, then, can be defined as the optimal setting of three related factors: economy, ease, and efficacy. To put it simply: are the time and resources spent on preparing and executing a grammar task justified in terms of its probable learning outcome?

The A-factor: Appropriacy

No class of learners is the same: not only are their needs, interests, level and goals going to vary, but their beliefs, attitudes and values will be different too. Thus, an activity that works for one group of learners – i.e. that fulfils the E-factor criteria – is not necessarily going to work for another. It may simply not be **appropriate**. Hence, any classroom activity must be evaluated not only according to criteria of efficiency, but also of appropriacy. Factors to consider when determining appropriacy include:

- the age of the learners
- their level
- the size of the group
- the constitution of the group, e.g. monolingual or multilingual
- what their needs are, e.g. to pass a public examination
- the learners' interests
- the available materials and resources
- the learners' previous learning experience and hence present expectations
- any cultural factors that might affect attitudes, e.g. their perception of the role and status of the teacher
- the educational context, e.g. private school or state school, at home or abroad

Activities that fail to take the above factors into account are unlikely to work. The age of the learners is very important. Research suggests that children are more disposed to language learning activities that incline towards acquisition rather than towards learning. That is, they are better at picking up language implicitly, rather than learning it as a system of explicit rules. Adult learners, on the other hand, may do better at activities which involve analysis and memorisation.

Cultural factors, too, will determine the success of classroom activities. Recently there have been a number of writers who have queried the appropriacy of indiscriminately and uncritically applying methodologies in contexts for which they were never designed. Communicative Language Teaching (CLT) has been a particular target of these criticisms. CLT values, among other things, **learner-centredness**, that is, giving the learners more responsibility and involvement in the learning process. This is often achieved through **discovery learning** activities (for example, where learners work out rules themselves) and through **group work** as opposed to the traditional **teacher-fronted** lesson. CLT also takes a relatively relaxed attitude towards accuracy, in the belief that meaning takes precedence over form. Finally, CLT has inherited the humanist view that language is an expression of personal meaning, rather than an expression of a common culture. Such notions, it is argued, derive from very Western beliefs about education and language. Its critics argue that CLT is an inappropriate methodology in those cultural contexts where the teacher is regarded as a fount of wisdom, and where accuracy is valued more highly than fluency.

Of course, no learning situation is static, and, with the right combination of consultation, negotiation, and learner training, even the most entrenched attitudes are susceptible to change. The teacher is therefore encouraged to be both adventurous as well as critical, when considering the activities in the chapters that follow.

Conclusions   In answer to the question 'Why teach grammar?' the following
reasons were advanced:

- the sentence-machine argument
- the fine-tuning argument
- the fossilisation argument
- the advance-organiser argument
- the discrete item argument
- the rule-of-law argument
- the learner expectations argument

There are some compelling reasons why not to teach grammar:

- the 'knowledge-how' argument
- the communication argument
- the acquisition argument
- the natural order argument
- the lexical chunks argument
- the learner expectations argument

To the arguments in favour should be added two more recent insights
from second language acquisition research. These are the notions of
focus on form and of grammar consciousness-raising. Together they
comprise:

- the paying-attention-to-form argument

On balance, the evidence suggests that there is a good case for a role
for grammar-focused teaching.

Grammar presentation and practice activities should be evaluated
according to:

- how efficient they are (the E-factor)
- how appropriate they are (the A-factor)

The efficiency of an activity is gauged by determining:

- its economy – how time-efficient is it?
- its ease – how easy is it to set up?
- its efficacy – is it consistent with good learning principles?

The appropriacy of an activity takes into account:

- learners' needs and interests
- learners' attitudes and expectations

It is these twin aims – efficiency and appropriacy – which underscore
the description and evaluation of the techniques outlined in the rest
of the book.

Looking ahead   The two chapters that follow look at contrasting ways that grammar
can be presented. The first of these is concerned with deductive
approaches, where the starting point is the grammar rule. The second
looks at inductive approaches, where the starting point is language
data.

How to teach grammar from rules

3

- **A deductive approach**
- **Rules and explanations**
- **Sample lesson 1: Using a rule explanation to teach question formation**
- **Sample lesson 2: Teaching *used to* using translation**
- **Sample lesson 3: Teaching articles using grammar worksheets**
- **Sample lesson 4: Teaching word order using a self-study grammar**

A deductive approach

First of all, here are two important definitions:

- a **deductive** approach starts with the presentation of a rule and is followed by examples in which the rule is applied
- an **inductive** approach starts with some examples from which a rule is inferred

An example of deductive learning might be that, on arriving in a country you have never been to before, you are told that as a rule people rub noses when greeting one another, and so you do exactly that. An example of inductive learning would be, on arriving in this same country, you observe several instances of people rubbing noses on meeting so you conclude that this is the custom, and proceed to do likewise. In place of the terms **deductive** and **inductive**, it may be easier to use the terms **rule-driven** learning and **discovery** learning respectively.

As we saw in Chapter 2 (page 22) the deductive (rule-driven) approach to language teaching is traditionally associated with Grammar-Translation. This is unfortunate because Grammar-Translation has had a bad press. There are in fact many other ways of incorporating deductive learning into the language classroom. We shall be looking at some of these later in this chapter.

The reasons why Grammar-Translation has fallen from favour are worth briefly reviewing. Typically, a grammar-translation lesson started with an explanation (usually in the learner's mother tongue) of a grammar point. Practice activities followed which involved translating sentences out of and into the target language. The problem is that, since classes were taught in the students' mother tongue, there was little opportunity for them to practise the target language. What practice they got involved only reading and writing, and little attention was given to speaking, including pronunciation. Moreover, the practice sentences were usually highly contrived and any texts that were used were treated solely as vehicles for grammar presentation.

However, it does not require a great deal of imagination to envisage a 'new, improved' version of Grammar-Translation in which many of its weaknesses have been righted. It is not the case, for example, that the whole lesson need be conducted in the students' mother tongue. Speaking (including work on pronunciation) and listening practice can easily be incorporated into the basic lesson framework, and the translation exercises could just as well involve authentic texts. What this approach does require is teachers with sufficient proficiency in both languages – the learners' language and the target language – to make it work. Needless to say, Grammar-Translation is not viable in multilingual classes.

It is important to stress that the deductive method is not necessarily dependent on translation. In fact, many popular student grammar practice books adopt a deductive approach, with all their explanations and exercises in English. For example: see the extract from *Grammar Practice for Intermediate Students* opposite.

Before looking at some examples of deductive (rule-driven) lessons, it might pay to summarise the arguments against and in favour of such an approach. To start with, here are some possible **disadvantages**:

- Starting the lesson with a grammar presentation may be off-putting for some students, especially younger ones. They may not have sufficient **metalanguage** (i.e. language used to talk about language such as grammar terminology). Or they may not be able to understand the concepts involved.
- Grammar explanation encourages a teacher-fronted, transmission-style classroom (see page 17); teacher explanation is often at the expense of student involvement and interaction.
- Explanation is seldom as memorable as other forms of presentation, such as demonstration.
- Such an approach encourages the belief that learning a language is simply a case of knowing the rules.

The **advantages** of a deductive approach are:

- It gets straight to the point, and can therefore be time-saving. Many rules – especially rules of form – can be more simply and quickly explained than elicited from examples. This will allow more time for practice and application.
- It respects the intelligence and maturity of many – especially adult – students, and acknowledges the role of cognitive processes in language acquisition.
- It confirms many students' expectations about classroom learning, particularly for those learners who have an analytical learning style.
- It allows the teacher to deal with language points as they come up, rather than having to anticipate them and prepare for them in advance.

Nouns, adjectives and adverbs

1 ⭐
Subject and object pronouns

Subject pronouns

I	you	he	she	it	we	you	they

Object pronouns

me	you	him	her	it	us	you	them

● The subject is the person or thing doing the action:
  ***I** left early.*
  ***She** went home.*
  ***We** said goodbye.*

● The object is the person or thing
  receiving the action:
  *She telephoned **me**.*
  *I hit **him**.*
  *We saw **her**.*

Write the correct *pronouns* for these
sentences:

1 . . . . telephoned yesterday. (she)
   She telephoned yesterday.
2 We watch . . . . for hours. (he)
   We watched him for hours.
3 Hasn't . . . . arrived yet? (she)
4 . . . . don't understand. (I)
5 Are you talking to . . . .? (I)
6 Don't ask . . . . doesn't know. (she/she)
7 This is Julia: . . . . have known . . . . for years. (we/she)
8 Nobody told . . . . the bus was leaving. (they)
9 Why didn't . . . . ask . . . . to come? (she/they)
10 Don't ask . . . . . Ask . . . . . (I/he)
11 . . . . think . . . . doesn't like . . . . . (I/he/I)
12 . . . . asked . . . . to invite . . . . . (they/he/we)

I left early.

(from Walker and Elsworth *Grammar Practice for Intermediate Students*,
Longman, 1986)

Rules and explanations

Many of the pros and cons of a rule-driven approach hinge on the quality of the actual rule explanation. This in turn depends on how user-friendly the rule is. In Chapter 1 (page 11) a distinction was made between a rule that a linguist might devise to describe a regularity of the grammar (a **descriptive** rule) and a rule that a teacher might give learners to apply (a **pedagogic** rule). The point was made that it is not often the case that a linguist's version of a rule will be appropriate in a classroom context, and there will inevitably be, therefore, some trade-off between the **truthfulness** of a rule and the pedagogical **worth** of a rule.

What, then, makes a rule a good rule? Michael Swan, author of teachers' and students' grammars, offers the following criteria:

- **Truth**: Rules should be true. While truthfulness may need to be compromised in the interests of clarity and simplicity, the rule must bear some resemblance to the reality it is describing.
- **Limitation**: Rules should show clearly what the limits are on the use of a given form. For example, to say simply that we use *will* to talk about the future is of little use to the learner since it doesn't show how *will* is different from other ways of talking about the future (e.g. *going to*).
- **Clarity**: Rules should be clear. Lack of clarity is often caused by ambiguity or obscure terminology. For example: 'Use *will* for spontaneous decisions; use *going to* for premeditated decisions.' To which a student responded, 'All my decisions are premeditated'.
- **Simplicity**: Rules should be simple. Lack of simplicity is caused by overburdening the rule with sub-categories and sub-sub-categories in order to cover all possible instances and account for all possible exceptions. There is a limit to the amount of exceptions a learner can remember.
- **Familiarity**: An explanation should try to make use of concepts already familiar to the learner. Few learners have specialised knowledge of grammar, although they may well be familiar with some basic terminology used to describe the grammar of their own language (e.g. conditional, infinitive, gerund). Most learners have a concept of tense (past, present, future), but will be less at home with concepts such as deontic and epistemic modality, for example.
- **Relevance**: A rule should answer only those questions that the student needs answered. These questions may vary according to the mother tongue of the learner. For example, Arabic speakers, who do not have an equivalent to the present perfect, may need a different treatment of this form than, say, French speakers, who have a similar structure to the English present perfect, but who use it slightly differently.

But rules are only one component of an explanation. Here, for example, is a procedure a teacher might use to give a grammar explanation (T = teacher; ST = student). In the right-hand column the different stages of the explanation are identified.

T:	Right. The past perfect.	(cueing)
T:	The past perfect is formed from the past of the auxiliary 'have', plus the past participle.	(rule of form)
T:	For example, 'everyone had left', 'the film had started'.	(examples)
T:	So, what's the past perfect of 'they go'?	(check)
ST:	'They had gone.'	
T:	Good.	
T:	It is used when you are talking about the past, and you want to refer to an earlier point in the past.	(rule of use)
T:	For example, 'We were late. When we got to the cinema, the film had already started.'	(example)
T:	Did the film start after we arrived, at the same time as we arrived, or before we arrived?	(check)
ST:	Before.	
T:	Right.	
T:	So, it's like this. [draws]	

b   a

———————|——————————|——————————————▶   (illustration)

T: We arrived at this point in time (a). But I
      need to refer to an earlier point in the past,
      when the film started, here (b).

Notice that the explanation is staged in two parts, the **rule of form** being dealt with before the **rule of use**. (Sometimes it may only be a rule of form that is being explained, for example, the form of past tense regular verbs.) Note also, how, in the example, the rules are exemplified and illustrated where possible, and that running checks are made on the state of the students' understanding. Note, finally, that the rule statements themselves attempt to fulfil the conditions of truth, clarity, simplicity etc, outlined above.

What follows are some different approaches to rule-led teaching. Following each sample lesson is a brief discussion of the principles that underpin it, and an evaluation in terms of its efficiency (the E-factor) and its appropriacy (the A-factor).

Sample lesson

Lesson 1: Using a rule explanation to teach question formation (Pre-intermediate)

In the presentation the teacher uses an illustrated explanation to highlight a feature of English syntax (word order). The same kind of presentation could be used, with a little adaptation, for teaching other syntactic structures such as the passive, reported speech, embedded questions (*Do you know where the bank is?*) or cleft sentences (*What I like about London is . . .*).

Step 1

The teacher writes on the board the sentence:

> The president phoned the Queen.

She asks students to identify the verb in the sentence (*phoned*). She then asks them to identify the subject of the sentence (*the president*); and, finally, the object (*the Queen*). She reminds students that English word order typically follows a subject – verb – object pattern (SVO).

Step 2

The teacher then erases *the president* and substitutes *someone*:

> Someone phoned the Queen.

She elicits, or – in the event of not being able to elicit it – she provides the question:

Who phoned the Queen?

She writes this question and the answer on the board. She numbers the exchange 1:

> Someone phoned the Queen.
>
> 1 Who phoned the Queen?
>   – The president.

She then returns to the original sentence:

The president phoned the Queen.

She rubs out *the Queen*, substituting *someone*:

> Someone phoned the Queen.
>
> 1 Who phoned the Queen?
>   – The president.
>
> The president phoned someone.

She elicits (or models) the question and its answer and writes them on the board:

> Someone phoned the Queen.
>
> 1 Who phoned the Queen?
>   – The president.
>
> The president phoned someone.
>
> 2 Who did the president phone?
>   – The Queen.

She then asks the students to study the two questions and to think about the difference between the subject question 1 and the object question 2.

1 Who phoned the Queen?
2 Who did the president phone?

Step 3
The teacher explains the difference, pointing out that to form questions about the subject of the sentence requires no change in word order:

> | S | V | O |
> |---|---|---|
> | Someone | phoned | the Queen. |
> | Who | phoned | the Queen? |

Whereas to form questions about parts of the sentence *after* the verb (in this case the object) does require a change in the standard word order. (This change in word order is called **inversion**. Inversion is a feature of English question forms, as in *Are you married?* In the case of our example, the inversion is achieved by unpacking the verb *phoned* into its components *did* + *phone* and then enlisting the auxiliary *did* to perform the inversion.) The whole process looks like this:

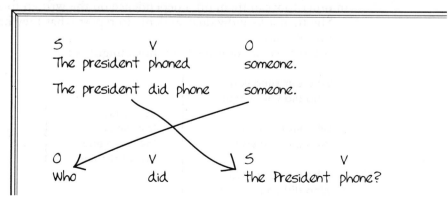

35

Step 4
The teacher then places four pictures of famous people (or, in the absence of pictures, their names) and connects them with arrows. For example:

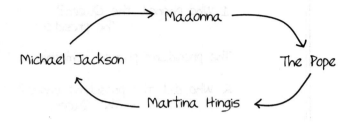

She explains that the arrows represent phone calls. She asks a variety of questions. For example:

> Who phoned Madonna?
> Who did Madonna phone?
> Who did the Pope phone?

She asks the students to continue this activity in pairs. She then invites them to make new 'phone networks' by changing the names of the people in the diagram, and to continue the question-and-answer activity.

For fun, she completes this activity by asking students: *Why did Madonna phone the Pope, do you think?* etc.

Step 5
The teacher writes on the board:

> Who phoned you yesterday/this morning/last weekend?
>
> Who did you phone yesterday/this morning/last weekend?

She asks the students to ask and answer the questions in pairs. As the students are doing this, she successively erases the questions from the board in order to wean them off a dependence on the written form.

She then asks individual students to report what they have found out to the whole class.

Alternative or additional questions might be:

Who e-mailed you		
Who did you e-mail		
	yesterday	
Who visited you	last week	
Who did you visit	last weekend	?
	last Christmas	
Who wrote to you		
Who did you write to		

Discussion

The success of a good explanation depends in part on the students' understanding of the **metalanguage**, i.e. the terminology used. The aim of Step 1, therefore, is to establish, from the outset, the terminology necessary to explain the difference between subject and object questions. Step 2 establishes a contrast between two grammatical forms, in this case, subject questions and object questions, with a view to raising the students' awareness of the difference. A similar contrast could be made between, for example, **active** and **passive** sentences:

> A man bit a dog.
> A dog was bitten by a man.

Or between **direct** and **reported speech**:

> He said, 'I am hungry.'
> He said he was hungry.

Or between two **aspects** of the same **tense** (see page 5):

> I read a book last night.
> I was reading a book last night.

The principal operating here is that it is often easier to establish a language rule in students' minds by contrasting two forms that are different in only one respect. These are known as **minimal grammar pairs**. (The same principle holds true for teaching pronunciation, e.g. by contrasting minimal pairs such as *ship* and *sheep*.) Note that the teacher asks the students simply to think about the difference, but not necessarily to verbalise it. Doing this gives the learner unpressured time in which to reflect on, and understand, the material being presented. Sometimes language learning is a silent activity. This does not necessarily mean it is passive.

In Step 3, having engaged the students' curiosity, and having primed them to be prepared for a grammar explanation, the teacher explains the language point. She also uses the board to provide a visual reinforcement of her explanation.

Step 4 is designed to test the learners' grasp of the rule, and to prepare them for independent practice. Notice that, initially, the students simply have to distinguish between the two sorts of question, without at this stage producing them. The exercise, restricted to the verb *phone*, is linguistically very controlled, so that learners are not overburdened with, for example, new vocabulary. They are free to devote maximum attention to the grammar contrast. The students are then allowed some less teacher-led practice, with the opportunity of providing their own content to the exercise. Step 5 continues in the direction of greater freedom and creativity, by offering the students a chance to personalise the language point. Also, by having them report on their findings, Step 5 encourages them to listen to each other, with a focus on meaning as much as on form.

Evaluation

The E-factor: The **efficiency** of this approach depends on the kind of rule being explained, and also on the teacher monitoring the learners' degree of comprehension at every stage of the explanation, and responding immediately to any problems they might have. If the rule is a relatively simple one then this approach can be extremely **economic** in terms of time. A simple rule might be one that involves a simple manipulation of elements, such as the active to passive operation, or one where there is a straightforward relation, with few or no exceptions, between a form and its use, such as the case of the third person *-s* on present simple verbs (*he works*). The grammar explanation approach is also very **easy**, in that it involves few if any materials and requires little or no preparation. It is therefore probably one of the most efficient ways of dealing with grammar problems that might arise in the course of a lesson as a result, for example, of a student's error.

There have been a number of research studies comparing the **efficacy** of deductive and inductive approaches to grammar teaching, but on the whole the results have been inconclusive. This is no doubt due to the number of variables involved, e.g. the students' preferred learning styles and the teacher's explanatory skills. A key factor seems to be the kind of item being taught. Some grammatical items seem to lend themselves to a deductive treatment, and others to an inductive one.

One problem in the **minimal pairs** approach to grammar presentation is the lack of context. The difference, for example, between:

> I read a book last night.
> I was reading a book last night.

may, in the absence of more context, be difficult for the students to locate, an issue that will be addressed in Chapter 5.

The A-factor: As has been pointed out earlier, the deductive approach is particularly **appropriate** for adult learners whose learning style and expectations predispose them to a more analytical and reflective approach to language learning. This of course means that it will not be suitable for learners who would rather learn through the experience of communicating. And it is particularly inappropriate for very young learners: abstract grammatical concepts such as subject, object and even verb, are beyond their grasp. Finally, whatever the style of the learners, over-prolonged 'chalk-and-talk' presentations will soon tire even the most attentive students. As a rule of thumb: the shorter the better.

Sample lesson

Lesson 2: Teaching *used to* using translation (Elementary)

In this lesson, the teacher has chosen to use translation to present *used to do* (as in *I used to go to the movies more than I do now*) to a group of Spanish-speakers. To follow this example it may help to know that the Spanish verb *soler* (present *suele*, past *solía*) means something like *to be accustomed to*.

Step 1

The teacher writes on the board:

> Tony solía fumar, pero lo dejó hace dos años.

He asks for an English translation, and, if not forthcoming, supplies this one:

Tony used to smoke but he stopped two years ago.

He then explains (in Spanish): 'To say you did something regularly, use *used to*. It means *solía*. For example, *Tony used to smoke*, or *Tony solía fumar*, which means that he doesn't smoke any more, it's finished, he quit.'

He then asks students how they would translate into Spanish a number of English sentences, provided orally, such as: *I used to eat meat; She used to go out with Alex; We didn't use to play tennis;* etc.

He then elicits English translations for Spanish sentences that he provides orally. For example: *Yo solía beber vino tinto* (*I used to drink red wine*); *José no solía fumar* (*José didn't use to smoke*).

Step 2

He then writes a sentence using the Spanish verb *soler* in its present tense form:

> Andy suele fumar un paquete entero cada día.

and asks for a translation. Students will probably assume that the English verb *used to* works in the present the same way that the Spanish verb *soler* does and they will attempt to translate the sentence as *Andy uses to smoke a packet a day* or *Andy is used to smoke* ...

He then explains (in Spanish) that *used to* has only past meaning, and has no present form. To translate *Andy suele fumar* ... one would need to say something like *Andy usually smokes* ..., *Andy is in the habit of smoking* ..., or simply *Andy smokes* ...

He follows up by asking students to provide English translations for sentences in either the past or the present, such as: *Teresa solía ir al gimnasio* (*Teresa used to go to the gym*); *Alberto suele ir de bici cada fin de semana* (*Alberto goes bike-riding every weekend*) etc.

Step 3

The teacher writes:

> I used to ski when I was young, but I stopped because it was too expensive.

He elicits a translation, and then erases key words, leaving:

I used to _____ when I was _____ , but I
stopped because _____ .

He asks students to write true sentences of their own using this model, to compare them in groups of three, and to ask and answer questions about the topics they have chosen.

Discussion

Although the teacher has chosen a relatively teacher-directed and board-focused means of presentation, he attempts to involve the learners at each stage, thereby reducing the danger of 'chalk-and-talkiness'. Moreover, explanations are kept short, and the presentation is illustrated with clear examples. The teacher is also aware of the hazards of translation, and takes care to anticipate these. It is not the case, for example, that every instance of the Spanish verb *soler* is translatable as *used to* – instances of one-to-one matches of grammatical structures across languages are comparatively rare. So, showing what a structure doesn't mean is as important as showing what it does mean – what was referred to (on page 32) as its **limitation**. To do this the teacher (in Step 2) sets a trap for the students: he deliberately encourages them to overgeneralise the common ground between *soler* and *used to*, so that he can then make his point about the fact that *used to* has no present tense form, thus anticipating an error that many students make. This trap-setting technique (also called 'leading the student up the garden path') has been shown to be an effective teaching strategy – more effective than structuring the presentation so that students are prevented from making the error, for example by not letting them talk about present as well as past habits.

Evaluation

The E-factor: In terms of **efficiency**, translation is probably the most **economical** means of conveying meaning – at least in terms of orienting learners towards a rough idea of the meaning – bearing in mind that translation is always only an approximation. And it is certainly easy, requiring no resources such as visual aids or texts, and therefore little or no preparation. All the teacher has to do is to anticipate instances where the students might overgeneralise, as in the case of the verb *soler*, and assume that the English equivalent behaves in exactly the same way. Why, then, has translation had such a bad press?

Perhaps the main drawback is in terms of **efficacy**. There is a widely held belief in the 'no-pain-no-gain' principle of language learning. That is, unless the learner has invested some mental effort in the process, the gains will be short-lived. Translation requires minimal mental processing, and hence loses in efficacy what it makes up for in ease and economy. Over-use of translation may also reduce the amount of exposure students get to the target language. As Berlitz put it, as long ago as 1911: 'In all translation methods, most of the time is taken up by explanations in the student's mother tongue, while but few words are spoken in the language to be learned. It is evident that such a procedure is contrary to common sense.'

The A-factor: Translation is of course only really possible in monolingual classes and where the teacher has a good command of the students' language. In these cases it often seems inappropriate *not* to use translation, given its speed and efficiency, and especially at elementary level where explanations in the target language may be over the heads of the students. A refusal to translate may also mean that learners make their own unmonitored and possibly incorrect translations. On the other hand, there may be students who will be disappointed by a high proportion of translation in the classroom, especially if they expect their teacher to provide them with a rich diet of the target language. This is one of the reasons, rightly or wrongly, that some students deliberately seek out native-speaker teachers.

Sample lesson

Lesson 3: Teaching articles using grammar worksheets (Upper intermediate)

Still within the framework of a rule-driven approach, the following procedure attempts to centre the teaching-learning process more on the students, with a view to a) giving them more responsibility for their learning, and b) providing more opportunities for real communication, even if the topic of conversation is grammar. The teacher has decided to deal with the English article system by dividing the class into groups and giving each group a different set of rules relating to article use.

Step 1

The teacher divides the class into three groups (or six or nine groups, depending on the class size), with three or four students in each group. She hands out an exercise sheet which requires students to complete the gaps in a text. Each gap represents a use of either the indefinite article (*a, an*) the definite article (*the*), or what is called the 'zero' article, that is, when no article is required before a noun, as in *I like ice cream*. Here is the beginning of the handout:

> **Articles**
> Complete the text by choosing the best word to complete the gap: *a*, *an*, *the*, or nothing. Sometimes more than one answer may be possible. If you are not sure about an answer, leave it: your classmates may be able to help you later.
>
> **Digestion**
> [1] _____ food we eat must be changed by [2] _____ body before it can be absorbed by [3] _____ blood and used to nourish [4] _____ cells of [5] _____ body. [6] _____ food is changed into [7] _____ nourishment by [8] _____ digestive system. [9] _____ digestion begins in [10] _____ mouth where [11] _____ food is chewed into [12] _____ small pieces and mixed with [13] _____ saliva before being … .

She asks the groups to work on this exercise, and gives them five minutes to do this. She then hands out three grammar summaries: A, B and C. Each grammar summary gives different information about the article system in English. Summary A covers some rules about when to use the definite article, summary B has rules about the indefinite article, and summary C has rules about the zero article.

Each group 1 gets summary A. Each group 2 gets summary B, and each group 3 gets summary C. Note that the groups do not see the grammar summaries of the other two groups.

The teacher then asks the students to study their grammar summary and to use it to help them complete the exercise, again working as a group.

Step 2
Once the students have had a chance to use the grammar summaries to help them do the exercise, the teacher re-groups them in such a way that the new groups comprise members of each of the original groups. One way of organising this is to number the students in each group:

> 1 2 3   1 2 3   1 2 3

and then to ask three number 1s to form a group, three number 2s another group, etc:

> 1 1 1   2 2 2   3 3 3

In their new groups, the students are instructed to compare their answers to the exercise, and to share any information from their grammar summaries that might help the other members in their group to complete the exercise. They are encouraged to explain their grammar information, rather than simply show their classmates the grammar sheets.

Step 3
The teacher then checks the exercise in open class, asking learners to justify their answers by reference to the rules on their worksheets.

Discussion

This lesson is based on the belief that, given the right incentive, learners can teach each other. To achieve this, it adopts the principle of the classic **jigsaw** activity. A jigsaw activity is an activity in which students have to do a task, but the information they need in order to do it is distributed amongst them in such a way that no one student has it all. This creates an **information gap**. Only through collaboration and the exchange of information can students complete the task. Such activities are a mainstay of communicative methodology (see page 18). They are a way of contriving communicative interaction. Normally the jigsawed information relates to real-life tasks, such as arranging a meeting, or deciding who was responsible for an accident. In this lesson the information that has been jigsawed is grammatical. To complete the task (i.e. the grammar exercise) learners will need to share the information, which in turn will involve speaking English. They are learning about the language and getting communicative practice at the same time. In fact, studies of learners doing this kind of exercise suggest that they do exactly that: they do just as well when tested on the grammar as do students taught more traditionally, and they speak just as much as students doing meaning-focused (i.e. not grammar-focused) information gap activities.

The teacher's role is limited to that of monitor, supervising the activity and being available to help sort out problems in interpreting the grammar summaries. In Step 1, the learners are given a chance to pit their wits against the exercise, and activate their current state of knowledge. This in turn creates a need to study the grammar information, and, in Step 2, to exchange this information. Any lingering problems in understanding the grammar summaries can be sorted out by the teacher in Step 3. The same kind of exercise can be done just as well by starting with two groups, or with four. The important thing is that the students have to communicate – and communicate about grammar.

Evaluation

The E-factor: This approach is only **economical** in terms of the time spent on it if the students are communicating in English, i.e. getting the fluency practice that is customarily the aim of communicative activities. As long as this is the case, they are killing two birds with one stone. Moreover, the mental work involved in explaining a grammar point to someone else is likely to have a more enduring effect on memory than simply reading the rules and doing the exercise. Having to teach something is a great way of learning it, as most teachers know. The **ease** factor needs also to be considered: preparation of grammar summaries and exercises can be time-consuming for the teacher. An alternative would be to supply the class with published student grammar reference books, and direct them to particular pages, so that different groups are studying different rules related to the same general area (e.g. the passive, conditionals, question formation). They then have to complete a task by sharing their understanding of the rules. Most coursebooks nowadays also have a grammar reference section, which can be used in the same way.

UNIT 108   Word order (1) – verb + object; place and time

A   *Verb + object*

The *verb* and the *object* of the verb normally go together. We do *not* usually put other words between them:

		verb +	*object*	
	I	like	children	very much. (*not* 'I like very much children')
	Did you	see	your friends	yesterday?
	Ann often	plays	tennis.	

Study these examples. Notice how the verb and the object go together each time:

- Do you **clean the house** every weekend? (*not* 'Do you clean every weekend the house?')
- Everybody **enjoyed the party** very much. (*not* 'Everybody enjoyed very much the party')
- Our guide **spoke English** fluently. (*not* '...spoke fluently English')
- I not only lost all my money – I also **lost my passport**. (*not* 'I lost also my passport')
- At the end of the street you'll **see a supermarket** on your left. (*not* '...see on your left a supermarket')

B   *Place* and *time*

Usually the *verb* and the *place* (where?) go together:
>   **go home**   **live in a city**   **walk to work** etc.

If the verb has an *object*, the place comes after the *verb + object*:
>   **take** somebody **home**   **meet** a friend **in the street**

Time (when? / how often? / how long?) normally goes after *place*:

		place +	*time*	
Tom walks		to work	every morning.	(*not* 'Tom walks every morning to work')
She has been		in Canada	since April.	
We arrived		at the airport	early.	

Study these examples. Notice how *time* goes after *place*:

- I'm going **to Paris on Monday**. (*not* 'I'm going on Monday to Paris')
- They have lived **in the same house for a long time**.
- Don't be late. Make sure you're **here by 8 o'clock**.
- Sarah gave me a lift **home after the party**.
- You really shouldn't go **to bed so late**.

It is often possible to put *time* at the beginning of the sentence:
- **On Monday** I'm going to Paris.
- **Every morning** Tom walks to work.

Some time words (for example, **always/never/often**) usually go with the verb in the middle of the sentence. See Unit 109.

216   Word order in questions → UNITS 48–49   Adjective order → UNIT 98   Word order (2) → UNIT 109

(from Murphy, R. *English Grammar in Use*, Cambridge University Press, 2nd edition 1994)

The A-factor: For classes who like talking about grammar, and who, at the same time, are happy to take some responsibility for their own learning, this approach is particularly **appropriate**. Conversely, students who would feel abandoned by the teacher, and who might be mistrustful of their colleagues' explanations, are likely to react negatively to such an approach, unless assured that the teacher will closely monitor the group work and be available for consultation.

Sample lesson

Lesson 4: Teaching word order using a self-study grammar (Intermediate)

Many students have access to self-study grammars – that is, grammar reference books which also include exercises and a key. These grammars are potential sources of learner-directed grammar learning, both in the classroom (as should be apparent from Sample lesson 3) and out of the classroom. In this sample lesson, the teacher exploits the self- and peer-instruction potential of grammar practice books to target a feature of syntax.

Step 1

The teacher has identified a common problem in the class – the tendency to put adverbials between subject and object, as in *I like very much techno music*. (The adverbial in this case is *very much*.) So he directs learners to Unit 108 in *English Grammar in Use* by Raymond Murphy (see opposite). The teacher tells them to study the grammar rules for homework, to do the exercise on the facing page (see 108.1 below), and to check it by reference to the answers in the back of the book. They are also asked to design – as a homework task – their own exercise along similar lines, by writing twelve original sentences, some of which are correct and some of which are

---

EXERCISES

108.1 *Is the word order right or wrong? Correct the ones that are wrong.*

1 Everybody enjoyed the party very much. ....RIGHT...
2 Tom walks every morning to work. ...WRONG: to work every morning...
3 Jim doesn't like very much football. ....
4 I drink three or four cups of coffee every morning. ....
5 I ate quickly my dinner and went out. ....
6 Are you going to invite to the party a lot of people? ....
7 I phoned Tom immediately after hearing the news. ....
8 Did you go late to bed last night? ....
9 Sue was here five minutes ago. Where is she now? ....
10 Did you learn a lot of things at school today? ....
11 I met on my way home a friend of mine. ....
12 I fell yesterday off my bicycle. ....

incorrect, but all of which are sentences about themselves or about other students in the class. For example,

> I take everyday the bus to school.
> Nicole doesn't like Chinese food very much.

The teacher reminds the learners that the sentences should be designed to test their classmates' grasp of the word order rules they are to study.

Step 2

In the next lesson, the teacher puts the students in pairs, and they each exchange the exercises they have prepared. Each does the exercise they have been given. That is, they read their partner's sentences and decide which are grammatically correct. They also correct the ones that are incorrect. They then return them to their partner for checking. The teacher is available for consultation and will attempt to resolve any problems that arise – where, for example, there are two possible correct answers.

Step 3

The teacher then rounds off this part of the lesson by eliciting the word order rules from the class.

Discussion

This is another example of 'helping the learners to help themselves'. By encouraging them to take advantage of self-study resources, the teacher is instilling habits of self-directed learning. Moreover, by setting the grammar study to do as a homework activity the teacher frees up valuable class time that might be put to more productive use, such as practice. Virtually any grammar area that is covered in the self-study books is appropriate for this kind of task. It is particularly useful for dealing with problem areas that arise in class, but that are not dealt with in the students' current syllabus. Having the students design their own exercise is a particularly important task, since this helps them to engage with the rule at a productive, not merely receptive, level. By personalising the exercise, it is made more memorable, and certainly more interesting for other students to do. It also allows for the possibility of some discussion of the content of the sentences (*Is it true that you don't like Chinese food, Nicole?*). Most self-study materials – including the workbooks usually published along with coursebooks – are suitable as a basis for student-designed exercises. Exercise types that are common in these kinds of materials are **gap-filling tasks** (as in the sample lesson above) using both sentences and texts, **ordering tasks** such as correcting the order of words in a sentence, **expansion tasks** which involve producing whole sentences or texts from prompt words, and **transformation tasks** which might involve transforming direct speech into reported speech, or active into passive sentences.

Evaluation

The E-factor: By having the students study the grammar as a homework task, the saving in class time makes this approach maximally **efficient**. The exercise-writing task acts as an incentive to study the grammar. At the same time, this exercise-writing task requires students to engage with the rules at a deeper level than conventional self-study exercises normally require, thus increasing the **efficacy** of this approach. Finally, the pair work activity in the subsequent lesson provides an opportunity for peer-teaching, so that even the student who hasn't done his or her homework has a chance of benefiting. As for the ease of this approach, it assumes that students have access to self-study grammars. In the absence of these, the grammar reference pages now found in most coursebooks would serve equally well.

The A-factor: Relying on students to take some responsibility for their own learning to the extent of putting free time aside to study grammar rules and design exercises may be asking a lot of certain students, especially those who would prefer the teacher to be the source of all grammar input. To work well, this kind of activity may need to be introduced to the students gradually, with the exercise-writing activity taking place initially in class, in pairs or groups, and under the close supervision of the teacher. Nevertheless, with motivated groups of adult students who appreciate the value of freeing class time for language practice rather than for language study, this approach has a lot in its favour.

Conclusions

In this chapter, the distinction was made between:
- deductive approaches to grammar, where the rule is given and then applied to examples
- inductive approaches, where the rule is discovered by generalising from examples

Among the advantages of using a deductive approach are these:
- it is direct, no-nonsense, and can be very efficient
- it respects students' intelligence, expectations, and learning style (if they are analytically inclined)

On the other hand, a deductive approach has the following dangers:
- it can be seen as dull, over-technical, and demotivating
- certain kinds of learners, including younger ones, may react negatively
- it encourages the belief that learning a language is simply a case of knowing the rules

A lot depends on how user-friendly the rules are. Characteristics of helpful rules include the following:
- truth – is the rule true?
- limitation – is it clear what the rule covers and what it doesn't?
- clarity – is it clearly expressed?
- simplicity – is it uncluttered with sub-rules and exceptions?
- familiarity – does it use concepts that the students are familiar with?
- relevance – is it a rule that reflects students' specific needs and problems?

A lot also depends on the teacher's presentation of the rule. An effective rule presentation will include the following features:

- it will be illustrated by examples
- it will be short
- students' understanding will be checked
- students will have an opportunity to personalise the rule

Procedures requiring learners to teach and test one another might be as effective as a teacher explanation. This way they get grammar explanation and communication practice at the same time.

Looking ahead   With that thought in mind, the next chapter looks at some approaches to the presentation of grammar that encourage learners to work out rules from examples – **inductive learning**. We will look at ways in which examples can be presented to the learner so that they are a) intelligible, and b) organised in such a way as to promote efficient learning.

How to teach grammar from examples

- **Inductive learning**
- **Pros and cons of an inductive approach**
- **Sample lesson 1: Teaching imperatives through actions**
- **Sample lesson 2: Teaching the present simple using realia**
- **Sample lesson 3: Teaching *should have done* using a generative situation**
- **Sample lesson 4: Teaching the difference between past simple and present perfect through minimal sentence pairs**
- **Sample lesson 5: Teaching verbs that take both infinitive and *-ing* forms, using concordance data**

Inductive learning

As we discussed in the last chapter there are basically two ways in which a learner can achieve understanding of a rule: the **deductive** (rule-driven) path and the **inductive** (rule-discovery) path. In the former, the grammar rule is presented and the learner engages with it through the study and manipulation of examples. In an inductive approach, on the other hand, without having met the rule, the learner studies examples and from these examples derives an understanding of the rule. Both approaches can, of course, lead on to further practice of the rule until applying it becomes automatic.

The inductive route would seem, on the face of it, to be the way one's first language is acquired: simply through exposure to a massive amount of input the regularities and patterns of the language become evident, independent of conscious study and explicit rule formulation. Induction, or learning through experience, is seen as the 'natural' route to learning, and, as we have seen in Chapter 2, is strongly identified with methods of second language instruction that model themselves on first language acquisition, such as the Direct Method and the Natural Approach. These **experiential** methods of instruction share a basic assumption that language data (or input) is best processed inductively and without recourse to translation. They differ, however, in the position they take as to how best this input should be selected and organised. They also take different positions with regard to how and how often the teacher should intervene.

At the non-intervention end of this spectrum is **natural language acquisition** – picking it up as you go along. After all, the most natural route to a second language bypasses the classroom altogether, and the best example of experiential learning is that of immersion in the foreign-language speaking community. There are well-documented case studies of learners who have succeeded spectacularly in such a situation, just as there are as many studies of learners who have failed dismally. A desire to simulate the total immersion experience was the inspiration behind the language immersion programmes for schoolchildren that are now widespread in many bilingual contexts, such as in Canada. While the results of these programmes are impressive, and have been used by theorists to support a 'zero-grammar' position, such as the Natural Approach, there are nevertheless significant gaps in the language competence of the learners who emerge from these programmes, suggesting that unfocused exposure to unorganised language data may not be in itself sufficient. Induction, to work best, it seems, requires more than random exposure: it needs the intervention of either the syllabus designer, the materials writer, or the teacher, or all three.

A much earlier attempt to simulate the way children acquire their first language was the Direct Method (see page 21). Designed to challenge the decidely unnatural and highly intellectual procedures of Grammar-Translation, the fundamental belief behind the Direct Method was that our first language is acquired through the process of forming associations between language and the real world. In Direct Method classes, therefore, the rules of the language are supposedly acquired out of the experience of understanding and repeating examples which have been systematically graded for difficulty and put into a clear context. Here is an example of a teacher's notes for a beginner's class teaching the present continuous:

> 1 Walk from one side of the classroom to the other, and, while you are walking, say two or three times to the class: <u>I am walking</u>. <u>I am walking</u>. <u>I am walking</u>.
> 2 Select a student. Tell him to walk across the room. Indicate that he must say the sentence as you did: <u>I am walking</u>. <u>I am walking</u>. <u>I am walking</u>.
> 3 Tell him to walk across the room again. Indicate that he must be silent and you say to the class: <u>He is walking</u>. (three times)
> 4 The class can next say it in chorus.

Notice that in this approach to grammar teaching it was not thought necessary to draw the learners' attention to an explicit statement of the grammar rule. It was considered sufficient to rely on the learners' unconscious processes to do the job.

A development of the 'I-am-walking' kind of Direct Method present-ation, but which incorporated drill routines borrowed from Audiolingualism (see Chapter 2, page 21), was the **generative situation**, a popular procedure in British language schools from the 1960s on (and associated with an approach that is sometimes called **Situational Language Teaching**). A generative situation is a situation which the teacher sets up in the lesson in order to 'generate' several example sentences of a structure. Here, for example, is a situation from *English in Situations* (O'Neill, Oxford University Press, 1970) designed to present *say* with reported speech:

---

ii. A factory needs workers. Yesterday Bill read their advertisement in the paper. It said these things:
"We are a very large firm, pay very high wages, and have a good pension-scheme."
Bill is at the factory today. He now knows that all those things are not true. At this moment he is saying these things to the manager:
"YOU SAID YOU WERE A VERY LARGE FIRM but you are really a small one!
YOU SAID YOU PAID HIGH WAGES but they are really very low.
YOU SAID YOU HAD A GOOD PENSION SCHEME. You really haven't one at all."

Notice that the situation generates three examples of the targeted structure.

In the introductory notes to the teacher, the rationale for this kind of presentation is summarised by the author: 'Class must have chance to gain insight into when to use pattern. Situations represent typical instances. From these, they can generalise about use of pattern. Teacher may also decide to give formal rule. However, this is not enough in itself ... Formal rules can be helpful but cannot be substituted for student's own insight.' (p. vii)

You will note that an explicit rule statement is now tolerated. This was not the case with either the Direct Method or Audiolingual approaches. This reflects a sea change in thinking that was precipitated by Noam Chomsky's claim that language, rather than being a habit structure, was instead **rule-governed creativity**. Greater tolerance of rules marked a return to a more cognitive approach to language teaching, which had until then been associated only with Grammar-Translation (as we saw in Chapter 3). Second language learning, far from being a kind of conditioned reflex, was once again regarded as a conscious intellectual endeavour.

Meanwhile, developments in educational theory were promoting the value of what came to be known as **discovery learning**. The principle underlying discovery learning is that, in the words of Pascal, several centuries earlier: 'People are generally better persuaded by the reasons which they themselves have discovered than by those which have come into the minds of others'.

Discovery learning involves cycles of trial and error, with guidance and feedback provided by the teacher. As an example, learners might be set this problem:

Study these two sets of sentences:

a   Chris has lived in Cape Town for ten years.
Andrew has been learning to drive for six months.

b   Wendy has lived in Edinburgh since 1995.
David has been out of work since January.

They are then invited to choose *for* or *since* to complete the following sentences:

1   Anna has been married ____ seven years.
2   Jeff has been studying French ____ 1990.

This is fairly straightforward. The next three test items, however, challenge the learner to refine their initial hypotheses, since the clues are not so easy to interpret:

3   Chris and Jim have been together ____ a long time.
4   I have been living here ____ last summer.
5   They have been going out together ____ they met five weeks ago.

A wrong answer to any of these examples requires the learner to look more closely at the examples to see what the conceptual difference is between sets **a** and **b**. Note that an important element in this sequence is the 'up-the-garden-path' procedure, whereby learners are 'tricked' into misapplying their developing rule systems, thereby getting negative feedback (*'No, that's wrong'*) which in turn forces them to re-think their initial hypothesis. Thus, learners who have formulated the rule that *for* is used with time expressions involving numbers and units (*ten years, six months*), may be misled into answering 4 and 5 with *for*. By provoking this kind of error, a guided discovery approach forestalls the learners' natural tendency to stick with their first – usually quick-and-easy – hypothesis. The learner needs to know not only that *Jeff has been married for four years* is right, but that *I have been living here for last summer* is not.

The principles of the guided discovery approach were originally intended for self-instruction as a part of the kind of programmes which were used in language laboratories. They were soon adapted for classroom use, and coursebooks promoting an inductive approach to language learning are now more or less standard. An example of an inductive presentation of the present simple from *New Wave 1* (Longman 1988) is shown opposite.

Successfully inferring patterns and rules from the study of language data depends not only on how the data is organised, but on the quality and quantity of the data itself. With the advent of large computerised databases of language (called **corpora**) the possibilities of an inductive approach have been amplified enormously. Not only do we now have available a larger and more representative range of examples, but the pattern-seeking can be done more reliably and much, much more rapidly. Corpus data are particularly useful in computing the frequency and typical co-occurrences of individual

---

5

Find the rule

Look at these sentences:

You **know** Norma and Joe, don't you?
They **work** every day.
Joe **talks** to tourists, and Norma **writes** letters.
We always **go** to their travel agency.
The agency **offers** tours to many different countries.
I **like** the service there too.

▶ There is a final **s** on the verb only with
  certain subjects. What are they?

☐ I ☐ you ☐ he ☐ she ☐ it ☐ we ☐ they

Now apply the rule!

Circle the right verb.

I **see/sees** Norma almost every day, or

she **call/calls** me. She and Joe sometimes

come/comes to my house on weekends.

Joe usually **tell/tells** us some funny stories.

(from Maple, R. *New Wave 1*, Longman, 1988)

words. One way of doing this is by means of **concordancing** programs. A concordance is a collection of the instances of a word or phrase, organised in such a way as to display its immediate linguistic environment. Look, for example, at the concordance below of the word *data* as it has appeared so far in this chapter. This concordance throws up one or two interesting facts, not least that (for this writer anyway) the word *data* can be used with both singular and plural verb forms (*the data is organised*; *Corpus data are ...*)

The potential of corpora as sources for discovery learning is still being debated: the advantage of having so much language data at one's fingertips has to be balanced against the danger of being overwhelmed, with the result

```
1    e and -ing form, using concordance  data  Inductive learning As we discu
2    e a basic assumption that language   data  (or input) is best processed i
3    d exposure to unorganized language   data  may not be in itself sufficien
4    les from the the study of language   data  depends not only on how the da
5    e data depends not only on how the   data  is organised, but on the quali
6    n the qualitiy and quantity of the   data  itself. With the advent of lar
7    h the advent of large computerised   data  bases of language (called corp
8    nd much, much more rapidly. Corpus   data  are particularly useful in com
```

that the learner can no longer see the wood for the trees. Nevertheless, concordances, often in modified form, are appearing more frequently in course-books, as, for example, this inductive exercise:

Grammar: *so . . . that/such . . . that*

1	It was **so embarrassing!** The, it was the Monday aft
2	ht. **I'm so tired I could go straight to bed.** I mana
3	**Are you so young that you can't even share?** I would
4	. **She's such a nice person.** Weren't they a lovely c
5	t? **It's such a shame that he's gone.** And put that s
6	It was **such a warm day I thought it could be nice.**

From the *British National Corpus* (Spoken)

1 Answer these questions about *so* and *such* in the sentences above.

1 Which word goes before an adjective on its own, *so* or *such*?
2 Which word goes before a noun, with or without an adjective?
3 Which sentences have two clauses/two main verbs? Is it necessary to start the second clause with *that*?

(from Mohamed, S. and Acklam, R. *Intermediate Choice*, Longman, 1995)

Pros and cons of an inductive approach

What are the advantages of encouraging learners to work rules out for themselves?

- Rules learners discover for themselves are more likely to fit their existing mental structures than rules they have been presented with. This in turn will make the rules more meaningful, memorable, and serviceable.
- The mental effort involved ensures a greater degree of **cognitive depth** which, again, ensures greater memorability.
- Students are more actively involved in the learning process, rather than being simply passive recipients: they are therefore likely to be more attentive and more motivated.
- It is an approach which favours pattern-recognition and problem-solving abilities which suggests that it is particularly suitable for learners who like this kind of challenge.
- If the problem-solving is done collaboratively, and in the target language, learners get the opportunity for extra language practice.
- Working things out for themselves prepares students for greater self-reliance and is therefore conducive to learner **autonomy**.

The disadvantages of an inductive approach include:

- The time and energy spent in working out rules may mislead students into believing that rules are the objective of language learning, rather than a means.
- The time taken to work out a rule may be at the expense of time spent in putting the rule to some sort of productive practice.
- Students may hypothesise the wrong rule, or their version of the rule may be either too broad or too narrow in its application: this is especially a

danger where there is no overt testing of their hypotheses, either through practice examples, or by eliciting an explicit statement of the rule.
- It can place heavy demands on teachers in planning a lesson. They need to select and organise the data carefully so as to guide learners to an accurate formulation of the rule, while also ensuring the data is intelligible.
- However carefully organised the data is, many language areas such as aspect and modality resist easy rule formulation.
- An inductive approach frustrates students who, by dint of their personal learning style or their past learning experience (or both), would prefer simply to be told the rule.

Research findings into the relative benefits of deductive and inductive methods have been inconclusive. Short term gains for deductive learning have been found, and there is some evidence to suggest that some kinds of language items are better 'given' than 'discovered'. Moreover, when surveyed, most learners tend to prefer deductive presentations of grammar. Nevertheless, once exposed to inductive approaches, there is often less resistance as the learners see the benefits of solving language problems themselves. Finally, the autonomy argument is not easily dismissed: the capacity to discern patterns and regularities in naturally occurring input would seem to be an invaluable tool for self-directed learning, and one, therefore, that might usefully be developed in the classroom.

Sample lesson

Lesson 1: Teaching imperatives through actions (Beginners)

The following presentation, while sharing similarities with the 'I-am-walking' procedures of the **Direct Method**, in fact borrows more from the **Total Physical Response** (TPR) method. TPR is based on the principle that learners learn best when they are wholly engaged (both physically and mentally) in the language learning process.

Step 1

The teacher asks two students to come to the front of the class, where there are three chairs placed in a row, facing the rest of the class. The teacher sits in the middle chair and the two students sit either side. To the two students he says *Stand up* and at the same time stands up himself, indicating with a gesture that the students should do the same. The teacher then says *Walk*, and walks across the room, indicating to the students to do the same. Further instructions follow: *Stop ... turn around ... walk ... stop ... turn around ... sit down*. Each time the teacher acts out the instruction and the students follow. When, by this means, they have returned to their seats, the teacher signals to the student on his left to remain seated. The sequence is then repeated, but this time only the student on the right performs the actions, following the instructions from the teacher, who, along with the other student, remains seated. When the student has successfully performed the instructions, it is the turn of the second student. This time the order of the instructions is slightly varied. The teacher next calls on one or two more students from the class to perform the set of instructions.

Step 2

The teacher teaches the names of various features of the classroom, such as *board*, *door*, *table*, *window*, *chair*, *floor*, *light*, simply by pointing to each one and saying its name a few times while students listen. With one student he then demonstrates, following a similar procedure as in Step 1, the instructions: *point to ...*, *walk to ...*, *touch ...*, *open ...*, and *close ...*, using as objects the classroom features previously taught. For example, *walk to the door*, *open the door*, *close the door*, *turn around*, *walk to the board*, *point to the window*, *touch the floor* ... The student performs the actions while the rest of the class watch. Further students act out similar sets of instructions given by the teacher, who gradually increases the number and density of instructions, so that students are soon having to listen to a complex set of instructions before they actually start to perform them.

Step 3

With one student the teacher then demonstrates the meaning of *Don't* ... by telling the student: *Stand up. Don't walk. Don't turn around. Sit down ...*, indicating when it is appropriate to perform the action and when not. Step 2 is then repeated, but with the inclusion of the negative imperative form *don't* ...

Step 4

The teacher writes the following table on the board. He reads sentences from it aloud, asking students to repeat them, before writing them down in their books.

(Don't) Stand up.	(Don't) Walk to the board.
Sit down.	Point to the light.
Walk.	Open the door.
Stop.	Close the window.
Turn around.	Touch the floor.

Discussion

Learning a language through actions attempts to simulate the experience of first language learning. Notice that in this TPR-style lesson there is no pressure on the learner to speak, a feature that differentiates TPR from its Direct Method antecedents, where the learners would normally have repeated the commands (see the *I am walking* example earlier in this chapter). The principle operating here is that, since children seem to develop listening competence in advance of the ability to speak, second language learners should do likewise. Moreover, this 'silent period' removes some of the stress associated with language learning, allowing the learner to concentrate solely on understanding the input without the requirement to produce accurate output. Notice, also, that the rule for formation of the imperative (including its negative form) is not overtly stated. The language data is simply organised in such a way so as to enable the learners to formulate the rule for themselves (Step 4).

Evaluation

The E-factor: Using actions to convey the meaning of grammatical items is highly efficient, since it requires little in the way of preparation, and by by-passing explanation or translation offers a direct route to the the learner's language processing capabilities – hence the 'directness' of the Direct Method. Moreover, proponents of Total Physical Response claim that physical movement engages holistic right-brain processes, a better basis for language acquisition than linear left-brain ones. At the same time the absence of the stress associated with the pressure to produce correct sentences reduces what is thought to be the main inhibitor to successful second-language learning. However, there are only a limited range of language items that lend themselves to physical demonstration and classroom enactment, imperatives being an obvious candidate. Others are prepositions of place, demonstratives (*this*, *that*), present progressive (*I am walking* ...) and such functional areas as commands, requests, and offers. The illustration of more subtle concepts may require considerable ingenuity.

The A-factor: While many students respond positively to activities with a performance component and appreciate the so-called **right to be silent**, there are others who may find this *Simon says* approach somewhat infantile, and react negatively. TPR activities are probably best used as one of several different procedures rather than being used exclusively, and are particularly suitable for younger learners or beginners. For adult learners, some advance explanation of the rationale underlying this approach might be a good idea.

Sample lesson

Lesson 2: Teaching the present simple using realia (Beginners)

Realia is the technical term for any real objects that are introduced into the classroom for teaching purposes. Thus, a word family such as the names of different fruits could be taught by using pictures of fruit, or they could be taught using realia – real fruit. In this presentation the teacher uses realia to elicit examples of the present simple in a beginners' class.

Step 1

The teacher shows the class a collection of objects that she says she found in a bag left in the teachers' room. They include such things as a bus pass; a programme for the current jazz festival; an empty glasses case; the guarantee for a well-known brand of watches; a novel in French; a swimming cap; a guitar pick; etc. (Note that none of the objects has the owner's name.) She divides the class into pairs and hands each pair an object, telling them they should try to work out some characteristics of the owner of that object, so that the teacher can work out who the bag belongs to and return it. The learners study their object and then pass it on to the pair on their left until they have had a chance to look at them all.

Step 2

The teacher asks the class: *Do you think it's a man or a woman?* Depending on their response the owner is thereafter referred to as *he* or *she* or *he/she*. She then elicits sentences from the learners based on their deductions. Vocabulary is provided as necessary and the sentences are 'shaped' by the teacher and written on to the board so as to display the target form clearly, which is the present simple form of the relevant verbs:

> He likes jazz.
> He takes the bus.
> He wears a Swatch.
> He wears glasses.
> He plays the guitar.
> He reads French.
> He goes swimming.

Step 3

The teacher directs attention to the form of the verbs, highlighting the final *-s*. She also checks that students are clear as to the time reference implied by this use of the present simple, by asking: *Is this past, present, or future?* To the answer *Present*, she responds: *Right now, or every day?* to elicit *Every day*.

She then rubs out the verbs, and asks learners to complete the list from memory, working in pairs. This task is then checked.

Step 4

The teacher then asks the students individually to write a similar list of sentences about a person in the class. The teacher monitors the sentence-writing stage, providing vocabulary where needed, and suggesting improvements. Individual students then read out their sentences, while the other students guess who is being described.

Discussion

Visual aids and realia are useful in that they circumvent the need for translation, and they can communicate a greater range of meanings than can actions. In this example, the teacher uses real objects to engage students' interest in a piece of detective work (Step 1). One problem here is that students may lack the necessary vocabulary to express their deductions. This may require the teacher to pre-teach the names of the individual objects (although this is not going to provide them with the verbs they will need). With a monolingual class, allowing the students to consult bilingual dictionaries is a possibility. Alternatively, the teacher simply cuts Step 1 short at the point where the students go into pairs, and provides the vocabulary at Step 2. The language-focus stage (Step 3) may make more or less use of grammatical terminology, according to the teacher's assessment of the class. The 'zero option' would be to leave the rule unstated, and simply move straight on to Step 4, on the assumption that the context has made the meaning obvious, and that there are sufficient examples for the students to work out the rule.

Evaluation

The E-factor: Collecting a sufficiently varied range of objects detracts from the **ease** of an approach that relies on realia, but this is perhaps compensated for in terms of **efficacy**: real objects engage students' interest, and hence heighten their attention.

The problem is that there is only a limited number of grammatical structures that lend themselves to this approach. At higher levels, for example, the same lesson could be adapted to teach the language of deduction: *He must wear glasses; he probably likes jazz; he almost certainly belongs to a gym.* Wrapped objects can be used to good effect to teach the language of perception: *It looks like a ...; it feels like a ...; it sounds like a ...* etc. The contents of someone's weekend bag could be used to teach either the present perfect (*She's been to the beach ...*) or future forms (*She's going to take a plane ...*). And a full shopping bag is an obvious choice for teaching the language of quantities, e.g. *how much?* and *how many?* However, the advantages in terms of engaging the learners' attention have to be balanced against the effort involved in preparation.

The A-factor: Adult learners may be wary of a style of teaching that harks back to the primary classroom, so the appropriacy of using realia needs to be carefully considered. At lower levels and for younger learners, however, it is a very direct way of dealing with meaning, and, especially where there is a problem-solving element, is quite compatible with serious language learning.

Sample lesson

Lesson 3: Teaching *should have done* using a generative situation (Intermediate)

The situational approach that follows was designed to overcome some of the shortcomings mentioned above of relying solely on demonstration, namely, that only a limited number of structures lend themselves to this approach. By offering the learner a context, it also avoids the problems involved in either excessive explanation or translation.

Step 1

By means of a picture on the board (a drawing, photo, or picture cut from a magazine) the teacher introduces a character she calls Andy. She draws a rough map of Australia, placing next to it a picture of a four-wheel drive vehicle. She elicits ideas as to how these pictures are connected, establishing the situation that Andy has decided to drive across the Australian desert from the east to the west. She elicits the sort of preparations a person would need to make for such a journey. Students suggest, for example, that Andy would need a map, a spare wheel, lots of water, a travelling companion, food, a first aid kit, and so on. The teacher selects some of these ideas, and writes them in a column on the board, and one or two ideas of her own:

```
To do this kind of journey, you should:

take a map
take water
not travel alone
advise the police
not travel in the wet season
```

Step 2

The teacher then explains that Andy made no preparations. He didn't take a map, he didn't take water, he travelled alone, etc. She asks the students to imagine what happened. Using their ideas as well as her own, she constructs the following story: Andy set off, got lost, got very thirsty, set off in search of help (leaving his vehicle behind), got trapped by sudden flood waters, etc. The police set out in search of him but couldn't find him because he had abandoned his vehicle and left no note. The teacher checks these facts by asking one or two students to recount them.

Step 3

The teacher asks the class: *Well, what do you think of Andy?*, eliciting answers like *He was stupid.* Teacher: *Why?* At this point, students may venture sentences, like *He must take a map.* Having thus established the idea of disapproval of past actions, the teacher models the sentence: *He should have taken a map*, repeating it two or three times. The students repeat the sentence in unison and then individually. The teacher reminds the students of the concept of disapproval by asking *Did he take a map? (No). Was that a good idea? (No) So ...?* The students respond: *He should have taken a map.*

She then repeats this process using the example of travelling alone, eliciting, modelling, drilling, and concept-checking the sentence: *He shouldn't have travelled alone.*

Further prompting elicits example sentences, such as:

He should've taken water.
He shouldn't have left his car.

At strategic points, the teacher recaps the sentences that have been generated, using the words on the board as prompts. So far, nothing has been written on the board.

Step 4

The teacher then clears the board and writes up the following table:

| He | should have | taken water. |
| | shouldn't have | travelled alone. |

60

She asks students, working in pairs, to add further sentences about the situation to the table. Individual students read sentences aloud from the table, and the teacher reminds them of the pronunciation of *should have* i.e. /ʃʊdəv/.

Step 5
The teacher then asks students to imagine the dialogue when the police finally find Andy. She writes the following exchange on the board:

```
Police:   You should've taken a map.
Andy:     I know I should. I didn't think.
```

Students, working in pairs, continue writing the dialogue along the same lines, and then practise it aloud, taking it in turns to be the police officer and Andy.

Discussion
The above example represents a type of grammar presentation procedure within which there is scope for many variations. For example, the situation (Step 1) can be introduced using board-drawings, magazine pictures, personal photos, or video. Alternatively, the situation could emerge out of a text the students have read or listened to. The point is that however it is established, the situation **generates** several examples of the targeted grammar item.

By eliciting some of the content of the presentation, the teacher aims both to involve the learners more actively in the lesson, and to monitor their developing understanding of both the situation and the target language. Likewise, some teachers might choose not to drill the example sentences (Step 3), but rather let the students silently reflect on them, in the belief that the mental and physical demands of immediate production distract attention from the brain work involved in working out the rules.

The number of examples of the targeted item is at the teacher's discretion. However, the more data the students have to work with, the greater the likelihood of their hypothesis being correct. But, in the interests of time and as this is only the presentation stage, four or five examples of a structure are probably sufficient.

The decision to withhold the written form (until Step 4) is based on the belief – inherited from Audiolingualism – that the written form might interfere with the correct pronunciation. However, it is likely that learners are going to make spelling-sound mismatches anyway, and perhaps the sooner that these are dealt with the better. Also, it is generally easier to pick up grammatical and lexical information from the written form than from the spoken, which suggests that, in the interests of rule induction, it may not be a good idea to withhold the written form too long.

Notice that in the example, no attempt is made by the teacher to elicit a statement of the rule. She relies instead on frequent checks of students' understanding of *should have done*. Nevertheless, this is no guarantee that learners will formulate the correct rule. Eliciting a statement of the rule (e.g. that *should have* is used to criticise past actions) might help, but this will depend on the learners' command of terminology. In a monolingual class, a translation of one or two of the examples could be elicited instead.

Evaluation

The E-factor: A situational context permits presentation of a wide range of language items. It is therefore more versatile than the 'I-am-walking' school of presentation, which relies solely on what can be demonstrated here-and-now. Furthermore, the situation serves as a means of contextualising the language and this helps clarify its meaning. At the same time the generated examples provide the learners with data for induction of the rules of form. Students can be involved in the development of the presentation as well as in solving the grammar 'problem': this makes it less dry than a traditional grammar explanation. Moreover, the situation, if well chosen, is likely to be more memorable than a simple explanation. All these factors suggest that this approach rates high in terms of **efficacy**.

But there are also problems, as was suggested earlier. What if the students don't 'get' the rule? Or what if they get the wrong rule? Wouldn't it have been easier to explain it from the start? What if the students don't realise it is a grammar presentation at all? If students are in the wrong mind-set they are unlikely to do the kind of cognitive work involved in the induction of grammar rules.

This kind of presentation also takes more time than an explanation. Time spent on presenting language is inevitably time spent at the expense of language practice, and it is arguable that what most students need (especially at intermediate level and beyond) is not the presentation of rules but opportunities to practise them. Thus, the generative situation loses points in terms of its **economy**. And it also requires a resourceful teacher who not only is able to conjure up situations that generate several structurally identical sentences, but who has also the means (and the time) to prepare the necessary visual aids. These factors detract from the **ease** of this approach.

The A-factor: The popularity of this kind of presentation owes a lot to the fact that it dispenses with the need for either translation or explanation. Translation and explanation were for a long time associated with traditional, transmission-style teaching, and translation is of course not feasible with multilingual classes. While many of the reservations about translation and explanation have been reassessed (see the previous chapter), the situational presentation is still popular, and is particularly appropriate with younger learners and with classes of beginners. However, given its relative inefficiency, it should probably be used cautiously with learners who are in a hurry, or who are at a level where lengthy and elaborate presentations might seem somewhat patronising.

Sample lesson

Lesson 4: Teaching the difference between past simple and present perfect through minimal sentence pairs (Pre-intermediate)

In this example the teacher is contrasting two easily confused verb structures. The class are familiar with both these structures but have met them only separately rather than in combination.

Step 1

The teacher writes the following three sets of sentences on the board:

> 1 a I've seen all of Jim Jarmusch's films.
>   b I saw his latest film last month.
>
> 2 a Since 1990, she's worked for three
>   different newspapers.
>   b She worked for The Observer in 1996.
>
> 3 a Have you ever been to Peru?
>   b When were you in Peru?

He asks the class first to identify the two verb structures in each of the sets, and establishes that each sentence **a** is an example of the present perfect, while each sentence **b** is an example of the past simple. If students are in any doubt about this, he quickly recaps the rules of form for each of these structures.

Step 2

He then asks the learners to consider the differences in meaning in each case (1–3), and to see if they can come up with a general rule for the difference between the present perfect and the past simple. He allows them to discuss this in pairs. In checking this task, he elicits the fact that the present perfect is used to talk about experience but without specifying when it happened. The past simple, on the other hand, is used to talk about a specific experience, often at a specified past time. To clarify this point, he draws the following timelines on the board and asks students to match them to the examples **a** or **b**.

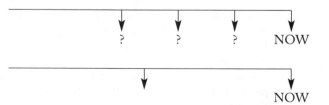

Step 3

He divides the class into pairs and sets them the following exercise which requires them to choose between the two forms:

> **a Complete this job interview between an Interviewer (I) and a Candidate (C). Put the verbs in brackets in the Present Perfect or Past Simple.**
>
> I: So, tell me a little about the things you . . . (do).
> C: Well, I . . . (study) French and German at university. Then, I . . . (teach) in secondary school for a few years.
> I: . . . you (enjoy) teaching?
> C: No, not really. I . . . (not like) the discipline problems. So, I . . . (start) working for a large drug company.
> I: . . . you (work) abroad at all?
> C: Yes, well about three years ago I . . . (get) a job in France, selling advertising space for a science magazine.
> I: . . . you (go) anywhere else?
> C: Yes, I . . . (work) in Germany in 1990.
> I: Oh really? What . . . (do) there?

(from Mohamed, S. and Acklam, R. *Pre-Intermediate Choice*, Longman, 1993)

Discussion

The assumption on which this presentation is based is that it is often easier to make sense of a concept when it is contrasted with a closely related concept. The **aspect** system of English (see page 5 for an explanation of aspect) lends itself to such contrasts, where the difference between, for example, *Have you seen my daughter?* and *Have you been seeing my daughter?* can have important implications. By presenting two sentences that are only different in one or two particulars (hence their name: **minimal pairs**), the teacher is better able to focus the students' attention on exactly how the choice of form determines a difference in meaning. However, in the absence of any contextual information there is a danger that the sentences become leached of meaning, and that the discussion of differences may become rather academic. The teacher needs to choose lexically simple examples with fairly self-evident contexts – sentences, in other words, that are not problematic in the way that authentic data can often be.

In Step 1, the teacher has presented the minimum number of paired sentences necessary to convey the target grammar contrast. (It often pays to have a few more in reserve.) As with all rule-explicit presentations, Step 2 demands a basic command of grammar terminology on the part of the learners. At lower levels and in monolingual groups, students might be permitted to formulate their hypotheses in their own language. The use of timelines provides a visual support for those students who might find a purely verbal explanation daunting. Hypotheses must be tested, and Step 3 is an essential stage in the presentation. It also shifts the focus back on to the learners.

Evaluation

The E-factor: The **minimal pairs** approach is designed to overcome the lack of **economy** of the generative situation (see sample lesson 3). By getting straight to the point, the minimal pairs presentation combines the best features of an **explanation-driven** approach (see Chapter 3) and a **discovery** approach. It is also relatively **easy** to plan and set up, and is therefore a useful way of dealing with problems as they arise. In terms of **efficacy**, it relies heavily on the choice of example sentences. More problematic still is the lack of context, which can sometimes lead students to the wrong conclusion, or, more frustratingly, to no conclusion at all. For example, apart from what they might already know about the two structures, there is nothing to help students untangle the difference between these two sentences:

a   They've been painting the kitchen.
b   They've painted the kitchen.

Whereas, with slightly more context, the difference in meaning starts to take shape:

a   'What a mess!'
     'Yes, they've been painting the kitchen.'
b   'The flat is looking nice.'
     'Yes, they've painted the kitchen.'

Students could waste a lot of time sorting out mistaken hypotheses unless the examples are well chosen and logically presented. Time spent sorting out wrong hypotheses can cancel out the advantage this approach has in terms of **economy**.

The A-factor: The direct and uncompromising grammar focus of this approach is particularly suitable for adult students who are not deterred by an analytical approach to language learning. By incorporating an element of discovery learning it can also foster collaboration in classes that work well together at problem-solving. Younger learners, or learners who prefer a more experiential approach to language learning, may find this approach to grammar dry and unmotivating, especially if the distinctions they are being asked to identify are not transparently obvious.

Sample lesson

Lesson 5: Teaching verbs that take both infinitive and *-ing* forms, using concordance data (Upper intermediate)

One persistent headache for learners is knowing which verbs in English are followed by the infinitive, as in *I've decided to resign*, and which verbs take the *-ing* form (sometimes called the gerund), as in *Have you finished eating?* The problem is complicated by the fact that there are a number of verbs that can take both forms, but with a (sometimes subtle) difference in meaning. In this lesson the teacher has decided to use concordance data to guide the students towards discovering these differences for themselves.

Step 1

The teacher divides the class into three groups (A, B, and C), and gives each group a different set of concordance lines as shown here:

Group A: *Remember*

REMEMBER (19:26, 07.05.98)

d Yanto, thoughtfully. On the other hand, I *remember* seeing them dancing together at a ball shortly before the month's Top to Tail if you own a poodle. *Remember* to listen out for Katie and friends on Radio 2. Should you here wasn't anyone to see me go. I *remember* thinking how white and cold her face looked, with ve food started to decrease in September, so *remember* to feed fish. Remember to check on them from time to ti t remember being so unhappy - not ever. I *remember* being in La Scala, Milan during the war. In the early 40s her to a colliery tip about four miles away. I *remember* going to a fruit and flower market in Leeds very early one what I can do but it's all working. Oh I must *remember* to take that film out. Is that the finish of it total? All I rem (which doesn't mean there weren't any). 'I *remember* seeing pictures of a fish like that at school, but I'm damn was working in Worcester. 'I don't seem to *remember* seeing you in church, Bridget,' said Clare. The last thing ber to feed him,' so I'll just have to *remember* to bring an electric drill up and see what I can do but it's a ehudi Menuhin was in town for a concert. I *remember* being rather keen on Bert when I was about fiteen. Whe

Group B: *Forget*

FORG?T (18.53, 07.05.98)

ernment last year announced that those who *forget* to flush public toilets will be fined up to US dollars. Results frothy fronds lit up by evening sun. I'll never *forget* seeing your Grandfather for the first time. I couldn't believe acting inspector over the weekend. I'll never *forget* being in hospital. s are getting shorter it doesn't mean you can *forget* having a bit of fun in the garden. Results of your search Yo othes. For instance, if you load Windows, but *forget* to take the mouse out of the bag, you can just clip the Tosh live alone. If you are leaving the area do not *forget* to pick up any clothes that are at the cleaners, or shoes, e, where shamrock fans forget to blur.Don't *forget* to put your clocks back tomorrow night. Once the removal o our or two watching TV together. She hadn't *forgotten* going to the pictures with Vernon to see The Song of Pa y solutions found for this query M. B. I never *forget* being called by a superintendent who said: 'Sergeant Bullo to add more volume of food daily. I must not *forget* to say something to the whole school about her.' Don't corr forget to bring music. 'Now eat up and don't *forget* to take your litter home with you.' If there is anything else yo

Group C: *Stop*

STOP (19.18, 07.05.98)

tense, listening. At the age of twelve, Bailey *stopped* eating meat. Although he had already taken his first mout though Anna was sure her mother had not *stopped* having baths or using perfume. Annabel was determined asthma? And it was two o'clock when they *stopped* talking, they stopped having their break! Results of your s s of Ron's hard training schedules. I finally *stopped* going to school when Charlie did, and Eva arranged for m ould appreciate it if the two gentlemen who *stopped* to help me when I had an accident with my car on the roa these last two days,' she told him when he *stopped* to greet her and ask if she had heard the brilliant spontan day I was filling up with petrol when a chap *stopped* to say he was a member of the Ferrari Owners Club and examine his reflection in the mirror. The bus *stopped* to pick up a passenger off one of the first terraced streets to the newspapers, but Mr Carter has never *stopped* believing he could solve the world's problems. But Joy defeat as gracefully as he could. Churchill *stopped* to take a cigar from the flap pocket of the one-piece siren he idea that had flitted through his mind. He *stopped* eating and reached across and took his wife's hand. I'd st

She tells the groups to study their lines, and divide them into two patterns. If they find this difficult she suggests that they look at the form of the verb that immediately follows the word in the central column of each set of lines. They are then instructed to try to work out the differences in meaning between the two patterns, still in their groups. The teacher monitors the group work, offering assistance where necessary.

Step 2
The teacher then re-groups the class, so that at least one member of each of the former groups A, B and C, is in each of the new groups. Their task is to explain to each other the patterns of form and meaning that they have found for their particular verb, and then, as a group, to work out a general rule that holds for all three verbs. They then report to the class.

Step 3
The teacher summarises by drawing the following timelines:

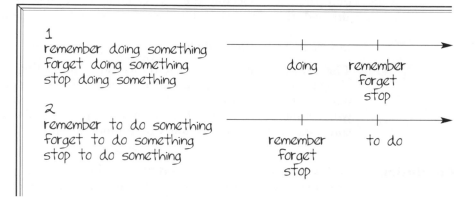

In other words, in the case of **1** the *doing* precedes the *remembering, forgetting, stopping*. In the case of **2** this sequence is reversed.

Step 4
To check their grasp of the rule, the teacher then hands out a discrimination exercise. For example:

1   I went to the post office but I forgot *to post/posting* the letter.
2   I don't remember *to see/seeing* the Millers at the party.

Discussion
The teacher has decided to split the data analysis task three ways, both to reduce the amount of data that learners have to sift through and to provide an element of information exchange, encouraging student interaction. Of course, it is not necessary to jigsaw the task like this. Nor does the data have to be authentic – it could be contrived or simplified, especially for lower levels. Finally, if learners have access to a computer room, the data could be provided in its 'raw' form, i.e. as a corpus of texts, and the students (assuming they are familiar with how to operate simple concordance software) could collect the concordance information themselves. The advantage of using computers is that it allows access to a greater number of concordance examples, and the examples themselves can be instantly re-sorted according to a variety of criteria.

Evaluation

The E-factor: In common with other rule-discovery approaches, it is necessary to balance the losses and gains that accrue when the learner is actively involved in the learning process. One loss might be the amount of time taken to work out the rules, but the gains will be the consequent improvement in terms of understanding. However, there are added costs that have to be taken into account when one is dealing with concordance data, one being the difficulty of understanding the concordance lines in their somewhat disembodied and truncated form, quite apart from the lexical problems thrown up by the use of authentic data. It may help to train learners to be able to understand and interpret concordance data – by, for example, talking them through one or two examples on overhead projector transparencies. Selecting the data carefully in advance is also a good idea, although this obviously will reduce the ease factor. Adopting this approach will of course depend on the teacher having access to concordancing software and a sufficiently large database to apply it to.

The A-factor: Learners unused to this way of presenting linguistic data are likely to be puzzled by it; the added challenge of working out rules may turn puzzlement into hostility. On the other hand, learners who are comfortable with computers, and are sufficiently motivated, may find that learning to use concordance data is an extremely useful tool.

Conclusions

In this chapter we have looked at a range of ways of presenting grammar that are designed to engage learners' inductive reasoning processes. That is, using a variety of means the teacher presents learners with pre-selected language data and encourages learners to work the rules out for themselves. As we have seen, these approaches are designed to offset the perceived weaknesses of deductive, rule-driven methods, and especially the lack of learner initiative associated with 'chalk-and-talk' approaches to teaching. Nevertheless, it should be clear from the above examples that inductive approaches vary markedly in terms of the role in which they cast both learner and teacher. On the one hand, there is the relatively passive and non-intellectual role of the learner in the TPR approach, while on the other there is the fairly teacher-independent and cognitively demanding approach using concordance data.

Looking ahead

A problem shared by the kinds of deductive and inductive approaches we have looked at in the last two chapters is their dependence on decontextualised and often very contrived examples of language. The next chapter looks at ways that attempt to remedy this by using chunks of language larger than the sentence.

5 How to teach grammar through texts

- **Texts and contexts**
- **Sources of texts**
- **Sample lesson 1: Using a scripted dialogue to teach the present simple**
- **Sample lesson 2: Using an authentic text to teach the passive**
- **Sample lesson 3: Using student language to review ways of talking about the future**
- **Sample lesson 4: Using a dictogloss to teach *would* for past habits**
- **Sample lesson 5: Using genre analysis to teach reporting language**

Texts and contexts

We are all familiar with the experience of being asked the meaning of a word and having to reply *But what's the context?* The very word *word* can mean different things in different contexts, as these examples show:

What does this word mean?
Can I have a word with you?
I give you my word.
Word has it that they are getting married.
If you want help, just say the word.
How should I word this letter?

Language is context-sensitive. This means that, in the absence of context, it is very difficult to recover the intended meaning of a single word or phrase. This is true of words taken out of the context of sentences. It is also true of sentences taken out of the context of texts. The following sentences are almost meaningless out of context:

1 The ones that don't, seem to think so.
2 It's a drink.

Here are the contexts from which these sentences were taken:

1 Is it important that a gin comes from London? The ones that don't, seem to think so. Because, though they all have 'London Dry Gin' on their labels, only one premium gin is actually distilled in London, the city of great gin making.

2 'Are you going to that Hodders party?'
I said that I didn't know anything about it.
'It's for that boring woman who writes picture books about Nash terraces. Every twit in London will be there.'
'So are you going?'
'It's a drink,' Musprat said, meaning yes.
(from Theroux, P. *Lady Max*, Granta 40)

The meaning of sentence 1 depends on references to the sentence immediately preceding it. The meaning of *It's a drink* in the second example depends on our expectation that what people say is relevant to what has just been said. In this case, the question *Are you going?* requires a relevant answer, which is likely to be either *yes* or *no*. It is more likely that *It's a drink* means *yes* rather than *no*, but notice that the author feels the need to make this interpretation explicit.

As decontextualised words and decontextualised sentences lose their meaning, so too do decontextualised texts. That is, texts divorced from their context may become difficult to interpret. Here are three short texts. Each is complete, in the sense that they are not extracts from larger texts, on which they might depend for sense (unlike the *It's a drink* example above). Nevertheless, in the absence of context, they are either ambiguous or unintelligible.

1 Port does not exist.
2 Only in Berkshire.
   Ken Stark, Leeds, Yorks.
3 To Wee Pig from Big Pig. Grunt! Grunt!

Number 1 is an instruction my computer gave me when I was trying to install a new printer. Number 2 is the response to a letter to the *Notes and Queries* section of *The Guardian* newspaper. (The original query was *Do dogs bark with regional accents?*) The third text also comes from *The Guardian*: it is a Saint Valentine's Day message printed on February 14th. In order to become fully intelligible all three texts require some knowledge of where, and even when, the text was originally placed. We need to distinguish, therefore, between the context of the surrounding **text** (as in the Paul Theroux extract) and the context of the surrounding **situation**. The first kind of context is sometimes called the co-text. The **co-text** is the rest of the text that surrounds and provides meaning to the individual language items in the text. The second kind of context is called the **context of situation**. Factors in the context of situation that are important to consider when interpreting the meaning of a language item are the roles and relationships of the speakers and the mode of communication (is it a public notice, a letter, a recorded message etc?). Finally, notice that the third text (the St Valentine's Day greeting) requires some understanding of the **culture** in which on a certain day of the year newspapers print messages of love from people pretending to be animals: this kind of context is called the **context of culture**. Lack of familiarity with features of the culture can seriously inhibit understanding.

One more point needs to be made before we look at the implications of these factors on the teaching of grammar. Although language has traditionally been analysed and taught at the level of the sentence, real language use seldom consists of sentences in isolation, but of groups of sentences (or, in the case of spoken language, groups of **utterances**) that form coherent texts. The term **text** will be used from now on to refer to both written and spoken English. Texts take many forms – postcards, novels, sermons, football commentaries, street signs, jokes, and air safety instructions are just a few. In real life we generally experience texts in their entirety and in their contexts of use. That is to say, we experience the whole joke and we usually experience it in a situation where joking is appropriate. It is a feature of classrooms, however, that language becomes detached from both its co-text and its context of situation. But, as we have seen above, once you start breaking texts up and relocating them, it becomes increasingly difficult to make sense of them.

The problem is that, just as it is easier to examine a fish out of water than in its natural habitat, so in order to look at grammar it is often easier to use examples taken out of context. This is particularly the case with beginner or elementary learners, for whom a natural context might be difficult to understand. But, as we have seen, taking words, sentences and texts out of context threatens their intelligibility. Taking individual grammar structures out of context is equally perilous. You might think you know what *He's playing tennis* means, that is, he is doing it now, as I speak. But only one of the following examples is consistent with that interpretation:

'Where's Tony?' 'He's playing tennis.'

He never wears his glasses when he's playing tennis.

Tomorrow morning he'll be in the office but in the afternoon he's playing tennis.

He's playing tennis a lot these days. Do you think he's lost his job?

There's this friend of mine, Tony. He's playing tennis one day. Suddenly he gets this shooting pain in his chest ...

What's more, the decontextualising of grammar often results in practice exercises that are of doubtful value. For example:

1 Choose the correct form of the verb:
   a Do you work/Are you working every weekend?
   b 'Cigarette?' 'No thanks, I'm not smoking/I don't smoke.'
   c 'What do you eat/are you eating?' 'Cake.'
2 Which of these sentences are grammatically correct?
   a I'm planning to go to India for my holidays.
   b 'The phone's ringing!' 'I'm going to get it!'
   c They will have a party next week.
   d I'm tired. I think I'm going to bed.

The point here is that none of these examples has a clear 'right answer' and a clear 'wrong' one. They are all well-formed sentences (that is, they are grammatically accurate), even though we recognise some choices as being more likely than others. But it is possible to imagine a context where, for example, *'Cigarette?' 'No thanks, I'm not smoking'* is perfectly appropriate. Questions of correctness are often unresolvable in the absence of context, and a lot of classroom time can be wasted arguing the toss over disembodied sentences. As someone once said: 'The confusions that occupy us arise when language is like an engine idling, not when it is doing work.' A text-based approach involves looking at language when it is 'doing work'.

Sources of texts

There are at least two implications to this text-level view of language. The first is that if learners are going to be able to make sense of grammar, they will need to be exposed to it in its contexts of use, and, at the very least, this means in **texts**. Secondly, if learners are to achieve a functional command of a second language, they will need to be able to understand and produce not just isolated sentences, but whole texts in that language. But a text-based approach to grammar is not without its problems. These problems relate principally to the choice of texts. There are at least four possible sources of texts: the **coursebook**; **authentic** sources, such as newspapers, songs, literary texts, the Internet, etc; the **teacher**; and the **students** themselves.

Coursebook texts tend to be specially tailored for ease of understanding and so as to display specific features of grammar. This often gives them a slightly unreal air, as in this example:

READING-TEXT NINE

This is Mr West. He has a bag in his left hand. Where is he standing? He is standing at the door of his house.

What is Mr West going to do? He is going to put his hand into his pocket. He is going to take a key out of his pocket. He is going to put the key into the lock.

(from Hornby, A.S. *Oxford Progressive English Course*, Oxford University Press, 1954)

Advocates of authentic texts argue that not only are such specially written EFL texts uninteresting – and therefore unmotivating – but they misrepresent the way the language is used in real-life contexts. On the other hand, the problems associated with authentic texts cannot be wished away, either, as any teacher who has attempted to use a dense newspaper article with low level students will have discovered. The linguistic load of unfamiliar vocabulary and syntactic complexity can make such texts impenetrable, and ultimately very demotivating.

A compromise position is to take authentic texts, and to simplify them in ways which retain their genuine flavour. This is the approach generally adopted by coursebook writers nowadays. Another alternative is to write classroom texts, but to make them more engaging than the example quoted above. In fact, with only the slightest change, the text about Mr West could be made somewhat more attention-grabbing:

> This is Mr West. He has a bag in his left hand. Where is he standing? He is standing at the door of his house. What is Mr West going to do? He is going to put his hand into his pocket. He is going to take a gun out of his pocket. He is going to point the gun at ...

One kind of authentic text – and one that has been largely under-exploited in conventional classroom practice – is the teacher's text. The teacher's story, the teacher's travel plans, the teacher's New Year resolutions, are likely to be of much more interest to the students than those of a character in a coursebook. The teacher has the added advantage of being able to talk to students in language they can understand, and to monitor their understanding 'on-line'.

And, finally, the students themselves are capable of producing text. The students' texts may be the most effective, since there is evidence to support the view that the topics that learners raise in the classroom are more likely to be remembered than those introduced by either teachers or coursebooks.

In the following sample lessons, we will see an example of how to deal with each of the four text sources (the coursebook, authentic texts, the teacher, the students). Further activities designed to exploit learners' texts (in the form of classroom conversation) and teachers' texts (e.g. narratives) are dealt with in Chapters 6 and 8 respectively.

Sample lesson

Lesson 1: Using a scripted dialogue to teach the present simple (Beginners)

The teacher has chosen the following recorded dialogue from a coursebook to use as a vehicle for introducing the present simple with adverbs of frequency (e.g. *usually*, *always*) to a group of beginners.

JOE: What do you do on weekends?

DAVID: Well, that depends. During the school year, I usually have to study on Saturdays.

J: And how about on Sundays?

D: Well, we always have lunch together, you know, the whole family. Then after lunch, I sometimes go to the park and meet my friends.

J: Oh? What do you do there?

D: We play soccer, take a walk, or just talk. After that, I go out. I usually go to the movies.

J: How often do you go out of the city?

D: About once a month. My uncle has a small farm in the mountains, so I sometimes drive up there.

J: That sounds nice. Do you go alone?

D: No, my mom, my two sisters and some of our friends usually go too.
J: But why do you go?
D: A lot of things: green trees, clean air, and no people.
J: Oh, just like LA!
D: Ha! That's a good joke.

(from Maple, R. *New Wave 1*, Longman, 1988)

Step 1
The teacher tells the class that she is going to play them a conversation between two friends. She asks students to close their books and to listen to the first part of the conversation and to answer this question: *What are they talking about: last weekend, next weekend, or every weekend?* She then plays the tape down to '*... and meet my friends.*' She allows the students to discuss with their neighbour the answer to her question, and offers to replay the section of tape if they wish.

Step 2
Once she has established that the conversation is about *every weekend* she asks the students to listen to the whole conversation and to put these words in the order that they hear them: *movies, drive, soccer, go out, study, lunch, park, walk.* (She checks that learners are familiar with these words.) She plays the whole conversation, allowing learners to check their answers with a neighbour, and she replays the tape if they seem to be having trouble with the task. She then checks the task, writing the words on the board in a list in the order they are mentioned on the tape. For the nouns in the list she elicits the appropriate verb and writes this up too. The list looks like this:

```
study
have lunch
go to the park
play soccer
take a walk
go out
go to the movies
drive
```

Step 3
She asks the students if they can tell her which of the activities in the list David does on Saturdays, on Sundays, and about once a month. She replays the conversation if necessary. She asks one or two other questions about the gist of the conversation, such as *Who does he have lunch with on Sundays? Why does he go to the farm? Who with?* etc.

Step 4
The teacher then asks learners to listen for the following words and to match them with the words in the list on the board: *usually, always,*

sometimes. She replays the tape as often as necessary, allowing students to check with their neighbour, and then she checks the task, writing the appropriate adverb against the word on the list on the board. For example:

usually   study
always   have lunch
sometimes   go to the park

Step 5
She then asks learners to focus their attention on two or three of these sentences and to tell her exactly what the speaker says. She replays the relevant sections of tape, until learners are able to provide the full sentence, which she writes on the board. For example:

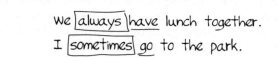

We |always| have lunch together.
I |sometimes| go to the park.

Step 6
The teacher draws the students' attention to the form of the structure, underlining the verbs and explaining that the present simple is used for routine activities. She draws a box around the adverbs (*always*, *sometimes* etc.) and points out that the adverb comes between the subject and the verb.

Step 7
She then asks learners to write two or three more sentences about David, using the above sentence pattern, i.e. subject + adverb + verb + ...

Step 8
She then asks the class to open their books, and she replays the conversation while they read, checking their answers to Step 7.

Step 9
She then invites the students to write four or five original sentences about themselves, using the pattern she has highlighted in Step 6.

Discussion
The first rule in using a text for the introduction of a new grammatical form is that the students understand the text. In this case, the teacher has chosen a text that she has estimated is within the students' range. At low levels this will usually mean a scripted text, i.e. one that has been specially written with learners in mind. She has also chosen a text with a high frequency of instances of the targeted grammar item. This will help learners **notice** the new item, and may lead them to work out the rules by induction (see Chapter 4).

But simply giving the students the chosen text is no guarantee that they will understand it. Steps 1 to 3 are the checking stage, during which the teacher guides the learners to a clearer understanding of the general gist of the text through a carefully staged series of tasks. Note that it is absolutely critical that the students realise that David is describing routine activities, as opposed to past or future ones. Unless this is checked, students might be misled into thinking that the target structure (present simple) is typically used to talk about the past or the future.

From Step 4 on she prepares students to home in on the target language: the instances in the text of present simple with adverbs of frequency. You will notice how, from Steps 1 to 5, each successive listening to the conversation requires learners to attend more and more closely to form. As a rule of thumb, listening tasks should generally move from a **meaning-focus** to a **form-focus**.

Having isolated and highlighted the structure in Steps 5 and 6, she then sets tasks that require learners to demonstrate their understanding of both the form and the meaning of the new item. Notice that at this production stage, the progression is from form-focus to meaning-focus. It is as if, having taken the language item out of its natural habitat (its context), the sooner it gets put back into a context, the better.

Evaluation

The E-factor: The **efficiency** of this kind of presentation depends very much on the text being within the learners' comprehension capacity, which is not always easy to gauge. It is also essential that the examples of the target language are both intelligible by reference to the context, and prominent or frequent enough in the text to be easily noticed. If such texts are unavailable they may have to be scripted and recorded by the teacher. This detracts from the **ease** of preparation. If texts are too long or too difficult, unpacking their meaning will require a lot of classroom time, reducing the **economy** factor. A further problem with texts tailored for language presentation is that they start to lose touch with reality, and fail to represent real language use. Coursebook texts have often been criticised on these grounds. However, assuming the texts are well chosen or well written, the contextual support they provide makes learning relatively easy, and this approach therefore scores highly in terms of **efficacy**.

The A-factor: Many learners will be familiar with materials that use texts to introduce and contextualise new items of language. Also, the use of dialogues generally matches learners' expectations of how language is used in the real world: people use language primarily to talk to each other. In this sense a text-driven approach is usually culturally appropriate. However, learners who experience difficulty in understanding recorded texts may find this approach frustrating. And, as with any inductive approach (see Chapter 4), discovering meaning in texts favours learners who are good at picking out patterns from examples. Learners who prefer a rule-driven approach may, however, feel that the use of texts is a rather roundabout route.

Sample lesson

Lesson 2: Using an authentic text to teach the passive (Intermediate)

This teacher has chosen the following authentic text, i.e. a text that was not written specifically for language teaching purposes, as a vehicle for introducing the passive:

> DOG ATTACK
>
> Jessica Johnson was out walking with her husband when she was attacked by an unsupervised Alsatian dog. Jessica's leg was bitten, and she had to have stitches in two wounds. Two days later, because the wounds had become infected, Jessica was admitted to hospital. Even after she was discharged, she needed further treatment from her GP – and she was told to rest for two weeks.
>
> Jessica is self-employed and her business was affected while she was sick. Also, the trousers and shoes she'd been wearing at the time of the attack were ruined by bloodstains, and had to be thrown away.
>
> Jessica told us, 'I'm now trying to get compensation from the owners of the dog.'

(from Axworthy, A. et al, *Which?* January 1991)

Step 1

Before handing out the text, the teacher tells the class the title of the article (DOG ATTACK) and asks the students in groups to think of and list vocabulary items that they might expect to find in such a text. These are written on the board, and the teacher uses this stage to feed in words from the text that might not have been mentioned by the students, e.g. *stitches, wounds, infected, bloodstains*.

Step 2

The teacher asks the class to read the text silently with a view to answering these questions: *Who was attacked? Where? How badly? Who was to blame?* The students check their answers in pairs before the teacher checks in open class. The teacher asks further questions about the text, such as *How long was she off work? What other losses did she suffer?*

Step 3

The teacher asks the class to turn the text over and then writes these two sentences on the board:

> 1 An unsupervised Alsatian dog attacked her.
> 2 She was attacked by an unsupervised Alsatian dog.

He asks the class if they can remember which of these two sentences was used in the text. He allows them to check the text if they cannot remember. He then elicits from the students a description of the difference in form between the two sentences, identifying 1 as an active construction and 2 as passive. He points out that while in 1 the subject of the verb (the dog) is the agent, or actor, in 2 the subject of the verb (she) is the person who is affected by the action. He elicits the structure of the passive sentence: subject +

auxiliary verb *to be* + past participle. He then asks the students to study the text again and decide why sentence 2 was considered appropriate in this context. He elicits the answer: *Because the woman is the topic, or theme, of the story, not the dog.* (Themes typically go at the beginning of sentences.)

Step 4
The teacher asks the students to find other examples of passive constructions in the text, to underline them, and to discuss in pairs or small groups the rationale for the use of the passive in each case. In checking this task in open class, the following points are made:

- The passive is typically used:
  1 to move the theme to the beginning of the sentence, and/or
  2 when the agent is unimportant, or not known.
- Where the agent is mentioned, '*by* + agent' is used.

Step 5
The teacher asks the students to cover the text and, working in pairs, to try and reconstruct it from memory. They then compare their versions with the original.

Step 6
The teacher asks students if they (or people they know) have had a similar experience. Having recounted their stories in English they are asked to write their story (or one of their classmate's stories) and this is checked for appropriate use of passive structures.

Discussion
The teacher has chosen a text which is both authentic and rich in examples of the passive. (It is not always the case, however, that grammar structures cluster in this way.) Because it is authentic rather than simplified, the teacher has to work a little harder to make it comprehensible, but, for the sake of presenting language in its context of use, this is an effort that is arguably worth making. As was pointed out above, authentic texts offer learners examples of real language use, undistorted by the heavy hand of the grammarian.

In Steps 1 and 2 the teacher aims to achieve a minimum level of understanding, without which any discussion of the targeted language would be pointless. As in Example 1, the shift of focus is from meaning to form, and it is in Step 3 that this shift is engineered. But even while the focus is on the form of the passive, the teacher is quick to remind students how and why it is used. To consolidate this relation between form and use he directs them back to the text (Step 4), which they use as a resource to expand their understanding of the passive. Note that there are one or two slippery examples in the text: is, for example, *the wounds had become infected* an example of the passive? In fact, strictly speaking, it is passive in meaning but not in form. Is *Jessica is self-employed* passive? This looks like a passive, but here *self-employed* is being used as an adjective. It is often the case that authentic materials throw up examples that resist neat categorisation. The teacher's choices here include: **a** removing these from the text, or re-phrasing them; **b** explaining why they are exceptions; **c** enlisting a more general rule that covers all these uses. Most experienced teachers would probably opt for plan **b**, in this instance.

Step 5 tests the ability of learners to produce the appropriate forms in context. The teacher has chosen a writing task rather than a speaking one, partly because the passive is not used in spoken English to the extent that it is in written English, but also because a writing exercise allows learners more thinking time, important when meeting relatively complex structures such as the passive. They then have a chance to personalise the theme through a speaking and writing activity (Step 6): the writing also serves as a way of testing whether the lesson's linguistic aim has been achieved.

Evaluation
The E-factor: This approach is **economical** only if the texts are neither too difficult nor too long, and if they contain typical examples of the target item. Therefore the time spent finding the right text, and, having found it, designing tasks to make it comprehensible, detracts from the **ease** of this approach. However, assuming the texts are available, this approach must rate highly in terms of **efficacy** for, apart from anything else, the experience of successfully learning grammar from authentic texts provides the self-directed learner with a powerful tool for independent study. Moreover, even if some learners are already familiar with the targeted item, authentic texts are usually so language-rich that the student is likely to come away from the lesson having gained in some other way, such as learning new vocabulary.

The A-factor: Students in many cultures will be familiar with text-based approaches to language study, and for many students the sense of achievement experienced from cracking an authentic text will be motivating. But others, especially at lower levels, may find them daunting. It may be better, in such cases, to use simplified texts.

Sample lesson

Lesson 3: Using student language to review ways of talking about the future (Intermediate)

For this lesson the teacher uses a cassette recorder with a microphone on an extendable lead. (She could also use a hand-held personal stereo that records.) She asks the small class of about six learners to sit in a closed circle; the microphone is placed in the centre of the circle; the teacher stands outside the circle and operates the cassette recorder herself.

Step 1
The teacher sets the topic: the coming mid-term holiday. She then waits while the students (who are familiar with this activity) construct and record a conversation, utterance by utterance. They do this as if they were having a natural conversation, taking turns, interrupting, changing topic, and so on, the only difference being that they pause to rehearse and record each 'turn' before the conversation resumes. The teacher's role is to provide the

language that the students need and to indicate when she thinks they are ready to record their turn.

A typical sequence might go like this:

ERNST (a student):	Ana, what will you do the next Easter holiday?
TEACHER:	Listen: *Ana, what are you going to do this Easter?*
ERNST:	Ana, what are you going to do this Easter?
TEACHER:	Good. Again. [She indicates she is going to record it.]
ERNST:	Ana, what are you going to do this Easter?
ANA (a student):	I don't know. Maybe I'll stay in the house.
TEACHER:	*At home.*
ANA:	I don't know. Maybe I'll stay at home.
TEACHER:	OK. [She indicates she is going to record it.]
ANA:	I don't know. Maybe I'll stay at home.
PAOLO (a student):	And you, Ernst, what are you going to do?
TEACHER:	Good. [She indicates she is going to record it.]
PAOLO:	And you, Ernst, what are you going to do?
ERNST (to teacher):	How do you say [he mimes skiing]?
TEACHER:	*I'm going to go skiing.*
ERNST:	I'm going to go skiing.
TEACHER:	OK. [She indicates she is going to record it.]
ERNST:	I'm going to go skiing.
etc.	

This produces the following amount of recorded text:

ERNST:	Ana, what are you going to do this Easter?
ANA:	I don't know. Maybe I'll stay at home.
PAOLO:	And you, Ernst, what are you going to do?
ERNST:	I'm going to go skiing.

Step 2

When the teacher – or the students – decide that there has been a fair spread of participation, and the conversation has run its course, the teacher directs the class to all face the board and the tape is rewound and replayed in its entirety. This allows students to appreciate the conversation as a piece of continuous text. Note that the amount of *recorded* material lasts for a much shorter time than the actual time spent preparing it. Twenty minutes of preparation may yield only two minutes of tape. The taped conversation is then transcribed on to the board. Any errors that got past the rehearsal stage are corrected.

Step 3

The teacher then draws the students' attention to features of the conversation that relate to the expression of future meaning. For example, she underlines the following:

Ana, what <u>are you going to do</u> this Easter?

I don't know. Maybe <u>I'll stay</u> in town.

She asks the learners to identify the different forms and to offer an explanation of their use in this context. For example, she guides them to the rule of thumb that *going to* is generally used to talk or ask about things already planned, whereas *will* is used at the decision-making stage itself.

Step 4

Students listen to the recorded text one more time, following it on the board. The teacher then rubs the text off the board and the students re-form in their original circle and improvise the conversation again from memory. They are encouraged to add more details if they wish.

Discussion

This procedure borrows heavily from a teaching method called **Community (or Counselling) Language Learning** (CLL) which was first promoted in the 1970s. CLL aims at centring the language learning experience as much as possible on the learners themselves, giving them responsibility for the content of the lesson, and engaging not only their intellects but their feelings as well. The teacher's role is essentially that of a consultant, providing the language the students need in order to express their meanings effectively, irrespective of the grammar agenda of the lesson (if there is one). There is no coursebook as such, nor even a syllabus: topics are initiated by the students and the teacher decides which language points to focus on from what emerges in the conversation and taking into account the level and needs of the class.

In the modified version of the CLL methodology as described above, the teacher, who in this case is working from a grammar syllabus, has pre-selected the theme so as to engineer instances of the 'structure of the day', i.e. future forms (Step 1). Certain structures lend themselves to this kind of thematic treatment: it's not difficult to imagine a topic that would throw up examples of the past tense, for example. But notice that the learners are not directed to use specific forms, by saying for example *I want you to use 'going to'*. The focus is very much on **meaning** from the outset.

The teacher reformulates rather than simply corrects what learners are trying to say. In other words, her attitude is not so much *That was wrong. This is what you should say*, as *I understand what you want to say. This is how I would say it*. The learners use the teacher as a kind of walking dictionary and reference grammar. At lower levels and in monolingual classrooms they would be permitted to express their meanings in their mother tongue and the teacher would then translate for them.

In Steps 2 and 3 the teacher takes a more directive role, transcribing the text (although there is no reason why individual students couldn't do this) and drawing the students' attention to features of the text. In orthodox CLL this means that the teacher needs to be able to make snap decisions as to what language items are appropriate to focus on. In our example, the teacher's job is made easier because the theme has been pre-selected to include examples of the targeted structures. The advantage of using the students' own text to focus on (rather than a coursebook or other pre-selected text), is that the teacher can be sure the students already understand it. Moreover, they may be more motivated to study the language in their own text rather than in a second-hand one.

Step 4 is a way of returning the text to the students, while at the same time providing an opportunity for a more fluid conversation.

Evaluation

The E-Factor: In terms of **ease** this technique rates high since it needs no planning nor any materials other than the recording equipment. Of course, the requirement to provide on-the-spot reformulations of what the students are trying to say can be fairly demanding, and is perhaps not recommended for novice teachers. In terms of time, it may not be the most **economical** way of giving grammar instruction, but the opportunity that the conversation stage provides for creative and personalised language use can have only positive side effects. The fact that the language focus emerges out of the learners' conversation means that there is a high level of relevance and therefore memorability. The **efficacy** of this approach is, therefore, high.

The A-factor: This technique is most **appropriate** for a group of about six students. If there are more than about nine or ten the amount each student can contribute tails off considerably. In classes where the students are reluctant either to take much initiative or to interact with one another, this technique is slow to get going. At beginner and elementary levels it requires the teacher to be fairly proficient in the learners' mother tongue, so it is unlikely to work well with low level multilingual classes. On the other hand, with small classes of either intermediate level students, or of monolingual beginners where there is a good class dynamic, this approach works very well if not used excessively.

Sample lesson

Lesson 4: Using a dictogloss to teach *would* for past habits (Upper intermediate)

A dictogloss is a form of dictation, but one in which the students hear and reconstruct the whole text, rather than doing so line by line.

The teacher has decided to use a spoken text as a context for *would* in its past habitual sense (e.g. *When we lived in Canada we would often go kayaking* ...). The technique he uses involves the students collaboratively reconstructing the text from memory and then comparing it with the original. Both the reconstruction phase and the comparison phase encourage a strong form focus – good for alerting students at this level to features of the language that might ordinarily pass them by.

Step 1

The teacher sets the theme by introducing the topic of summer holidays. After chatting about this for a few minutes, he then says 'I am going to tell you about how I spent my summer holidays as a child in Australia. I want you to listen and, as soon as I have finished, I want you to write down any words, phrases or sentences that you can remember.' He then tells them the following:

> 'When I was a child we used to go camping every summer. We'd choose a different place each year, and we'd drive around until we found a beach we liked. Then we'd pitch our tent, as near as possible to the beach. We'd usually spend most of the time on the beach or exploring the country round about. We never went to the same beach twice.'

Step 2

At a cue from the teacher, the students individually write down as much as they can recall, whether it be individual words or groups of words. The teacher then tells the class, working in groups of three, that he wants them to compare with each other what they have noted down, and to try and reconstruct the text. During this stage he is available to answer questions about vocabulary, e.g. *pitch a tent*, but does not intervene in the construction of the text.

Step 3

The teacher chooses a student to act as the class 'scribe' and to write their reconstructed version of the text on one half of the board, incorporating the suggestions of all the students in the class. Again, the teacher does not intervene at all, unless to answer relatively minor questions about vocabulary and spelling.

This is an example of a text that the students might produce collaboratively:

> When I was a child we used to go to camping in the summer. We choosed a different place each year.
> We drove until we found a beach which we liked. Then we pitched a tent, as near to the beach as possible.
> We used to spend most of the time on the beach or exploring the country around. We never went to the same beach twice.

Step 4

The teacher then projects an overhead transparency of his original text (or, in the event of not having an overhead projector, writes it on the board, next to the students' reconstructed version), and asks them to identify any differences between the two texts. They are quick to notice differences in word order and the substitution of *used to* for *usually* in the second-to-last sentence. They are slower to notice the four contracted forms of *would* (*we'd choose ... we'd drive ...* etc). The teacher challenges them to explain what these represent and individual students hazard a guess that they are examples of the past perfect, or of the second conditional. The teacher gently rejects these explanations, and briefly explains the use of *would* to express past habits.

Step 5
The students write their own texts, of a similar length and style, about their own childhood holidays, which they then exchange and discuss.

Discussion

The technique on which this lesson is based is variously called **dictogloss**, **dictocomp**, or **grammar dictation**. Unlike traditional dictation, where the text is read and transcribed clause-by-clause or sentence-by-sentence, the dictogloss technique requires learners to process the whole text at once. To do this, they have to capture the meaning of the text, although they may not be able to recall the exact forms in which that meaning is conveyed. That is, they understand the teacher's account of his holidays, but they don't have a word-for-word memory of exactly what he said. So, when it comes to reconstructing the meaning of the text, they tend to draw on forms which they are already familiar with (e.g. *we drove* rather than *we'd drive*). When they compare their version of the text with the original version, they are well-positioned to notice the difference between how they expressed the meaning and how the teacher himself expressed it. The difference between *we drove* and *we'd drive* is one instance of the difference between their grammar and the teacher's (or target) grammar. It is important for the learner to notice the differences for themselves, as we have seen before, in order for them to make the necessary adjustments to their mental grammar.

It is essential, therefore, that the text should be short, and within their general level of competence – apart, that is, from the inclusion of the targeted language form. For this activity, therefore, prepared texts will probably work better than authentic ones. But the delivery should aim for authenticity, and, if possible, the teacher should try to 'tell' the text at Step 1 rather than simply read it aloud, in order to engage the students' attention more directly. It may be necessary to re-tell the text once or twice: the teacher will need to monitor his students carefully in order to assess their comprehension.

It is also important that learners are given a chance to collaborate on the reconstruction task at Steps 2 and 3: the discussions they have at this stage about the appropriacy and accuracy of language forms are a valuable awareness-raising opportunity.

Step 4 is facilitated by the use of an overhead projector, but this is not essential. The teacher could write up his own version, or distribute it in the form of a handout. It is important that learners are clear as to the nature of the differences between their own text and the original. That is, their version may include acceptable alternatives (*a beach which we liked* for *a beach we liked*), or parts of it may be unacceptable (*we used to go to camping* for *we used to go camping*). Learners should be encouraged to ask questions about their texts in order to clarify the nature of these differences.

Evaluation

The E-Factor: The role of **noticing** as a prerequisite for learning has been emphasised in the recent literature on second language acquisition (see page 16), and the dictogloss technique provides a useful means for guiding learners towards **noticing the gap** between their present language competence and their target competence. It also allows learners at different levels to notice different things. Therefore, on the grounds of **efficacy** it rates high. It is also relatively **easy** to set up, although not all structures can be worked into a short text so naturally. In terms of **economy** the activity makes good use of time, and ensures learners are working collaboratively on language production tasks at an early stage in the lesson.

The A-factor: Some learners find the challenge of reconstructing texts from memory forbiddingly difficult, especially if they view it as a test rather than a learning exercise. Such learners need to be prepared gradually for dicto-gloss tasks, by means of using very short texts (even single sentences), or texts that they have already seen in their written form. The teacher can also allow them repeated hearings and can give them some explanation as to the purposes of the task, and suggests strategies they can use to perform it.

Sample lesson

Lesson 5: Using genre analysis to teach reporting language (Intermediate)

Language is context-sensitive, as we have seen. To understand language we need to have some knowledge of its context. Context can also determine the kind of language that is used. For example, a request for a loan will be worded differently if it is made to a friend rather than to a bank manager. The study of the ways in which social contexts impact upon language choices is called genre analysis. A **genre** is a type of text whose overall structure and whose grammatical and lexical features have been determined by the contexts in which it is used, and which over time have become institutionalised.

In this lesson, the teacher is using a relatively recent genre – the Internet news bulletin – to teach ways in which news is reported.

Step 1

The teacher dictates the following words to the class, and explains that they are the key words in a news story. The students are encouraged to ask about the meaning of any unfamiliar words and then, in pairs, to try to imagine what the story is about:

monkey	escaped	Thursday
zoo	missing	spokesman
enclosure	attacked	staff
vandals	loose	says
sighting	children's	night
twelve		

Step 2

Having elicited some of the students' predictions, the teacher presents the following authentic texts to the class and establishes that they are separate news bulletins taken at different times from an Internet website (TVNZ Website). She asks the students to try to put the three texts in the probable chronological order in which they appeared.

A

TODAY'S NEWS
Concern for missing monkey

Staff at a New Plymouth zoo say they are becoming concerned about the safety of a missing monkey.

The capuchin monkey escaped from the Brooklands Children's Zoo on Thursday night after vandals attacked its enclosure.

Zoo spokesman Anthony Joines says staff say they are particularly worried the monkey might eat something poisonous.

B

TODAY'S NEWS
Sighting of missing monkey

There has been a sighting of the monkey missing from a New Plymouth zoo.

Twelve capuchin monkeys escaped from the Brooklands Children's Zoo after vandals attacked their enclosure on Thursday night. All but one have been recaptured.

Zoo spokesman Anthony Joines says the monkey was seen near the zoo yesterday. He says as soon as there is another sighting, a team will head into the bush to search for it.

C

TODAY'S NEWS
Monkey still on the loose

The hunt continues in New Plymouth for a monkey missing from a zoo.

The capuchin monkey has been on the loose since vandals attacked its enclosure at the Brooklands Children's Zoo on Thursday night. All 12 monkeys in the enclosure got out but zoo staff managed to catch 11 yesterday.

Zoo spokesman Anthony Joines says the monkey will be able to survive on leaves, berries and bark, but it will be getting lonely.

Step 3

The teacher checks this task, drawing attention to clues in the text. For example, the use of the indefinite article in *a monkey* in the first sentence of texts A and C, suggests that it pre-dates references to *the monkey* in text B. The greater concern for the monkey's well-being in text A suggests that it follows text C. And, in fact, the actual order is C, A, B.

Step 4

The teacher then asks the students to use the evidence of all three texts to generalise the function of each paragraph. These functions are summarised briefly as being:

Paragraph 1: to report the current situation or most recent event, i.e. the UPDATE
Paragraph 2: to sketch the BACKGROUND to the story
Paragraph 3: to report an insider's VIEWPOINT

Step 5

The teacher asks learners to use the evidence of all three texts to identify the language features of each paragraph. Again, these can be summarised as:

UPDATE: present tenses (either present simple, continuous or perfect)
BACKGROUND: mainly past simple
VIEWPOINT: indirect speech; modal verbs (*will*, *might*)

Step 6

The teacher asks learners to imagine the outcome of the story, and to write the fourth and final news bulletin. They are reminded to use the pattern UPDATE – BACKGROUND – VIEWPOINT, and to choose their tenses accordingly. Students work in groups. One group doing this activity produced the following story:

> Joy for monkey's capture
> Staff at the New Plymouth zoo have been able to catch the monkey missing.
> This monkey was on the loose because some vandals attacked the monkeys' enclosure on Thursday night. Eleven of the twelve which escaped could be caught quickly.
> Zoo spokesman Anthony Joines says staff is very happy and he thanks citizens for their help. He hopes it never happens again.

Step 7
The teacher supplies students with the final story as actually reported.

TODAY'S NEWS

Escaped monkey shot dead

The monkey that has been on the loose in New Plymouth for five days has been shot dead.

The capuchin monkey was the last of 12 which escaped after vandals attacked an enclosure at Brooklands Children's Zoo.

Zoo spokesman Anthony Joines says the monkey was spotted in nearby Pukekura Park and a bid was made to try to coax it to take food laced with sedatives. However he says it became clear the monkey had no intention of going near staff and it was decided to shoot it.

Discussion

A **genre** is a text-type whose features have become conventionalised over time. A sports commentary, an e-mail message, a political speech, and (as in the texts we have just been looking at) an Internet news bulletin are all examples of different genres. Instances of a genre share common characteristics, such as their overall organisation, their degree of formality, and their grammatical features. These characteristics distinguish them from other genres. A **genre analysis** approach not only respects the integrity of the whole text but regards the features of a text as being directly influenced by its communicative function and its context of use. Thus, the way the text is organised, and the way choices are made at the level of grammar and vocabulary, will be determined by such factors as the relationship between speaker and listener (or reader and writer), the topic, the medium (e.g. spoken or written), and the purpose of the exchange. For example, the 'monkey' text would take a different form if it were a phone conversation between the zoo owners and the police, reporting the incident. The implication of a genre analysis approach is that grammatical choices are not arbitrary but are dependent on higher order decisions, e.g. the kind of text, the audience, the topic. Whereas traditionally it has been the custom to teach grammar independently of its contexts of use, a genre analysis approach sees grammar as subservient to the text and its social function. It is therefore best taught and practised as just another feature of that kind of text.

As in all text-based presentation, it is essential that students have a clear grasp of what the texts are about. The prediction task (Step 1) and the ordering task (Steps 2 and 3) are means to this end. (In this instance, getting the right order is of less importance than the fact that the task forces students to attend very closely to meaning.) The advantage of having several examples of this particular genre allows the teacher to guide the students to discovering its generic features (Steps 4 and 5), including such grammar items as the use of present tenses, past simple and modality. These grammatical features are treated, not as ends in themselves, but as choices determined by the nature of the genre. It is important, therefore, to relate them to the function of each paragraph and to show how each paragraph relates to the overall function of the text: i.e. breaking news. This is why the text begins not with the background but with the update. This in turn determines the use of present tenses in the first sentence. Step 6 provides students with an opportunity to apply these features in the construction of a whole text: they can also mine the previous three texts for other generic features.

Evaluation

The E-factor: Because a genre analysis approach takes a text-level view of language, it takes on board many more features than simply grammatical ones, and this suggests that it is very **economical**. However, there is a danger that the lesson can turn into all analysis and no synthesis. That is, too much time can be spent identifying and explaining features of the text that no time is left to use these discoveries to create new texts. Also, it is not always **easy** to find texts that are both representative of a genre and also at a level accessible to any but advanced learners. The **efficacy** of such an approach will depend on how easily text features can be pulled out of their contexts and highlighted. Where there is more than one example of a genre, as in the sample lesson above, this is much easier since all the teacher has to do is to ask the learners to compare the texts and find features that they have in common.

The A-factor: Where learners' needs can be fairly accurately predicted, a genre analysis approach will probably be very useful, especially for preparing them for formal genres such as business presentations or academic essays. General English students, especially at lower levels, may find the amount of language data overwhelming, and hence find it difficult to see the wood for the trees. They may also find it somewhat contrived to be producing examples of genres that are – like news bulletins – fairly specialised. Nevertheless, it could be argued that, even if students never have to produce texts such as news bulletins, the exercise of writing one will make them better readers of such texts, and, by paying greater attention to the overall structure and function of texts in general they will become better writers.

Conclusions

In this chapter we have discussed the way that:
- language is context-sensitive; which is to say that an utterance becomes fully intelligible only when it is placed in its context; and
- there are at least three levels or layers of context: the co-text (that is, the surrounding text); the context of situation (that is, the situation in which the text is used); and the context of culture (that is, the culturally significant features of the situation). Each of these types of context can contribute to the meaning of the text.

The implications of this context-sensitive view of language on grammar teaching are that:
- Grammar is best taught and practised in context.
- This means using whole texts as contexts for grammar teaching.

We have looked at a number of ways of using texts. Some of the advantages of using texts are the following:
- They provide co-textual information, allowing learners to deduce the meaning of unfamiliar grammatical items from the co-text.
- If the texts are authentic they can show how the item is used in real communication.
- As well as grammar input, texts provide vocabulary input, skills practice, and exposure to features of text organisation.
- Their use in the classroom is good preparation for independent study.
- If the texts come from the students themselves, they may be more engaging and their language features therefore more memorable.

Texts are not without their problems, however. Notably:
- The difficulty of the text, especially an authentic one, may mean that some of the above advantages are lost.
- The alternative – to use simplified texts – may give a misleading impression as to how the language item is naturally used, again defeating the purpose of using texts.
- Not all texts will be of equal interest to students.
- Students who want quick answers to simple questions may consider the use of texts to be the 'scenic route' to language awareness, and would prefer a quicker, more direct route instead.

Looking ahead   No single method of grammar presentation is going to be appropriate for all grammar items, nor for all learners, nor for all learning contexts. A lot will also depend on the kind of practice opportunities that the teacher provides. In the next chapter we will look at a range of practice types.

6 How to practise grammar

- Practice
- Accuracy
- Fluency
- Restructuring
- Sample lesson 1: Practising *how much/how many?* using a sequence of oral drills
- Sample lesson 2: Practising the third conditional using written exercises
- Sample lesson 3: Practising *can* using an information gap activity
- Sample lesson 4: Practising the present perfect using a personalisation task
- Sample lesson 5: Practising the passive using a grammar interpretation activity
- Sample lesson 6: Practising *going to* using conversation

Practice
So far we have been looking at ways of *presenting* grammar. But, as with any skill, simply knowing what to do is no guarantee that you will be able to do it, or that you will be able to do it well. Teachers will be familiar with learners who are fast and fluent speakers, but whose language is practically unintelligible because of the errors they make. There are also learners whose language is virtually error free, but who are painful to interact with because the production of every word is a struggle. A happy balance would be learners who are able to fine-tune their output so as to make it intelligible but who, at the same time, are equipped with a core of readily available, fairly automatic, language, so that they can cope with the pressures of real-time communication. It is the purpose of practice activities to target these two objectives: **precision** at applying the system, and **automisation** of the system. These two objectives are called, respectively, **accuracy** and **fluency**.

There is a third type of student: the one who is reasonably intelligible and at the same time fluent, but who can express only a relatively limited range of meanings. If such students are going to make any headway in the language, it is not enough simply to be able to speak fast and accurately.

91

They also need to be able to reorganise (or **restructure**) what they know in order to make it more complex. Practice activities may also provide this kind of learning opportunity: through practising the grammar, learners come up against situations which force them to reorganise their current knowledge. So, a third objective of practice is directed at **restructuring** – at integrating new knowledge into old.

Accuracy

To achieve accuracy the learner needs to devote some attention to **form**, i.e. to 'getting it right'. Attention is a limited commodity, and speaking in a second language is a very demanding skill. Learners have only limited attentional resources, and it is often difficult for them to focus on form and meaning at the same time. There is inevitably some trade-off between the two. So, for learners to be able to devote attention to form, it helps if they are not worrying too much about meaning. That suggests that practice activities focused on accuracy might work best if learners are already familiar with the meanings they are expressing. This, in turn, suggests that expecting learners to be accurate with newly presented grammar is a tall order. It may be the case that accuracy practice should come later in the process, when learners have been thoroughly familiarised with the new material through, for example, reading and listening tasks.

As we said, accuracy requires attention. Attention needs time. Research suggests that learners are more accurate the more time they have available. They can use this time to plan, monitor and fine-tune their output. Therefore rushing students through accuracy practice activities may be counterproductive. Classroom activities traditionally associated with accuracy, such as drilling, may not in fact help accuracy that much, especially where learners are being drilled in newly presented material.

Finally, learners need to value accuracy. That is, they need to see that without it, they risk being unintelligible. This means that they need unambiguous feedback when they make mistakes that threaten intelligibility. By correcting learners' errors, teachers not only provide this feedback, but they convey the message that accuracy is important. Knowing they are being carefully monitored often helps learners pay more attention to form.

To summarise, then, a practice activity which is good for improving accuracy will have these characteristics:

- **Attention to form**: the practice activity should motivate learners to want to be accurate, and they should not be so focused on what they are saying that they have no left-over attention to allocate to how they are saying it.
- **Familiarity**: learners need to be familiar with the language that they are trying to get right.
- **Thinking time**: monitoring for accuracy is easier and therefore more successful if there is sufficient time available to think and reflect.
- **Feedback**: learners need unambiguous messages as to how accurate they are – this traditionally takes the form of correction.

Fluency   Fluency is a skill: it is the ability to process language speedily and easily. Fluency develops as the learner learns to **automise** knowledge. One way they do this is to use pre-assembled **chunks** of language. Chunks may be picked up as single units, in much the same way as individual words are learned. Common expressions like *What's the matter?* and *D'you know what I mean?* are typically learned as chunks. Chunks may also be acquired when utterances are first assembled according to grammar rules, and then later automised. Fluency activities are aimed at this process of automisation.

Too much attention to form may jeopardise fluency. So practice activities aimed at developing fluency need to divert attention away from form. One way of doing this is to design practice tasks where the focus is primarily on **meaning**. By requiring learners to focus on what they are saying, less attention is available to dwell on how they are saying it. In this way, the conditions for automisation are created.

One way of engineering a focus on meaning is through the use of **information gap** tasks. Real communication is motivated by the need to bridge gaps: I need to know something – you have the information – I ask you and you tell me. In information gap tasks the production of language is motivated by a communicative **purpose**, rather than by the need to display grammar knowledge for its own sake. A communicative purpose might be: to find something out, or to get someone to do something, or to offer to do something. It follows that the exchange is a **reciprocal** one – there is as much a need to listen as there is to speak. This, in turn, means that speakers have to be mutually intelligible (not always a condition in drill-type activities). Furthermore, there is an element of the **unpredictable** involved – what if you don't have the answer I am looking for, or you refuse my request, or you reject my offer?

All these elements – purposefulness, reciprocity, mutual intelligibility, and unpredictability – are features of real-life communication. Classroom tasks that incorporate these features are known as **communicative tasks** and help prepare students for the cut-and-thrust of real communication. But more than that – because they are message-focused they serve to shift the learner's attention away from a concern for form, and in this way they help develop fluency.

To summarise: where **fluency** is the goal, practice activities should have these characteristics:

*   **Attention to meaning**: the practice activity should encourage learners to pay attention less to the form of what they are saying (which may slow them down) and more to the meaning.
*   **Authenticity**: the activity should attempt to simulate the psychological conditions of real-life language use. That is, the learner should be producing and interpreting language under real-time constraints, and with a measure of unpredictability.
*   **Communicative purpose**: to help meet these last two conditions, the activity should have a communicative purpose. That is, there should be a built-in need to interact.

- **Chunking**: at least some of the language the learners are practising should be in the form of short memorisable chunks which can be automised.
- **Repetition**: for automisation to occur, the practice activity should have an element of built-in repetition, so that learners produce a high volume of the targeted forms.

Restructuring   Restructuring involves integrating new information into old. Traditionally, restructuring was meant to happen at the **presentation** stage. That is, learners were expected to learn a new rule, and straightaway incorporate it into their 'mental grammar'. More recently there has been some scepticism as to whether this really happens. There is a growing belief that restructuring can occur during **practice** activities. One school of thought argues that communicative activities (such as information gap tasks) provide a fertile site for restructuring. This is because such activities **problematise** learning: what if you don't understand my question, or I don't understand your answer? This communication breakdown forces the learner to take stock and re-think. In turn it offers the potential for **negotiation**. Negotiation of meaning – the collaborative work done to make the message comprehensible – is thought to trigger restructuring. In fact, some early proponents of the communicative approach considered that this was all that was necessary for language acquisition to take place.

Restructuring is sometimes experienced by learners as a kind of flash of understanding, but more often, and less dramatically, it is the dawning realisation that they have moved up another notch in terms of their command of the language.

Practice activities designed to aid restructuring might have these characteristics:

- **Problematising**: having to deal with a problem often seems to trigger restructuring. For example, when learners are put in a situation where the message they are trying to convey is misinterpreted, they may be forced to reassess their grasp of a rule. Moreover, the input they get as they negotiate the meaning of what they are trying to express may also help reorganise the state of their mental grammar.
- **Push**: the activity should push learners to 'out-perform their competence' – that is, to produce or understand language that is a notch more complex than they would normally produce or understand.
- **Scaffolding**: there should be sufficient support (or **scaffolding**) to provide the security to take risks with the language. This means the practice activity should try to balance the new with the familiar. Scaffolding could, for example, take the form of telling a familiar story but from a different perspective. Teachers often provide students with scaffolding in the way they interact with them, repeating, rephrasing or expanding what they are saying in order to carry on a conversation.

Few practice tasks, whether their objective is accuracy, fluency, or restructuring, are likely to meet all of the criteria listed above. On the other hand, some tasks may incorporate features that suit them to more than one objective, e.g. both fluency and accuracy. Not all learners will respond in the same way to the same activity: differences in ability, learning style and motivation will affect the degree to which they engage with the task. This suggests that teachers need to be familiar with a fairly wide repertoire of practice activities. It also suggests that time spent in presenting new language should not be at the expense of time that could be spent on providing a useful variety of practice activities.

Sample lesson

Sample lesson 1: Practising *how much/how many?* using a sequence of oral drills (Elementary)

Grammar practice is often associated with drilling. In this example, the teacher of an elementary class has presented *how much?* and *how many?* with uncountable and countable nouns respectively, and is now providing practice through a sequence of different types of drills.

Step 1
The teacher says the following sentence two or three times:

How much milk have we got?

At a given signal, the class repeats this in chorus. Then the teacher indicates to individual students to repeat it. He corrects pronunciation where necessary.

Step 2
The teacher repeats the sentence and the class choruses it again. Then the teacher supplies the prompt:

rice

and indicates to a student to supply the response:

How much rice have we got?

The teacher supplies further prompts, such as *meat, juice, sugar, spaghetti* etc, and individual students provide the correct response. Note that all the examples (*meat, juice* etc.) are uncountable – i.e. they do not normally have a plural form.

Step 3
The teacher repeats Step 2, but this time uses pictures (of meat, juice etc.) rather than word prompts.

Step 4
The teacher repeats Step 1, but this time with the sentence:

How many bananas have we got?

The teacher then supplies prompts that are countable nouns, such as *potatoes, eggs, onions, tomatoes* etc. Initially the prompts are words, and then pictures.

Step 5

The teacher then supplies prompts that are a mixture of countable and uncountable nouns, first words and then pictures. For example:

TEACHER:	eggs
STUDENT 1:	How many eggs have we got?
TEACHER:	meat
STUDENT 2:	How much meat have we got?
TEACHER:	coffee
STUDENT 3:	How much coffee have we got?
TEACHER:	apples
STUDENT 4:	How many apples have we got?
etc.	

Step 6

The teacher distributes pictures to the students, who in pairs test each other.

Discussion

This sequence represents a classic progression through very controlled to less controlled drills. Notice that 'control' has two senses here: the language is controlled, that is, the learners have no choice in the language they are using; and the interaction is controlled, that is (until Stage 6 at least) the teacher dictates who speaks and when. These two types of control were considered essential in audiolingual practice if learners were to gain control (a third sense of the word) over the targeted sentence pattern.

Step 1 is an example of an **imitation drill**, in which the students simply repeat the teacher's model, first in chorus and then individually. Step 2 is a **simple substitution drill**, in which one element of the model is replaced by an item that fills the same slot. Note that it is in fact not necessary to understand the meaning of the slot-filling items at this stage. This is why the teacher introduces visual prompts (Step 3), which direct some attention on to meaning.

Step 4 repeats the process with a contrasting sentence pattern: *how many?* as opposed to *how much?* Step 5 brings the two patterns together and requires the students to make the countable/uncountable distinction so as to be able to make the necessary adjustments to the structure. This kind of drill is called a **variable substitution drill**, in that the response will vary, according to the prompt. Again, to ensure students really are attending to meaning, pictures are substituted for words. In Step 6, the teacher, satisfied that students have a measure of control over the distinction between *how much?* and *how many?*, relaxes control of the interaction, and allows the students to practise in pairs, thereby increasing the quantity of practice they are getting.

Evaluation

The E-factor: Drilling is **easy** to do, once students are used to it and the teacher has mastered a few basic techniques such as giving a clear indication as to when an individual response, as opposed to a class one, is required.

Some planning time needs to be given to the choice of prompts, and the use of pictures can be a drain on preparation time, but on the whole drilling is one of the easiest techniques to learn. It is also an **economical** way of practising grammar, since it requires little effort on the part of the teacher but quite a lot on the part of the students, especially if the drill is of the variable substitution type. It also allows the teacher to attend very closely to the accuracy of students' responses. Finally, drilling has wide applicability, in that almost anything can be drilled.

The **efficacy** of drills, however, is more questionable: as was pointed out earlier, drills are traditionally associated with accuracy practice and typically follow close on the heels of grammar presentation. This may be asking a lot of learners, however, since the enforced production of newly met items may deflect attention away from the brain work that is necessary for restructuring to take place. In other words, the requirement of 'getting their tongues round it' may be at the expense of 'getting their minds round it'. Drills may be more effective for fine-tuning language that learners are already fairly familiar with. Drills could thus come at the end of a teaching cycle rather than at the beginning, and act as a means of tidying up language that is still a bit ragged.

Another purpose drills may serve is to aid automisation of language chunks. In this sense, they are really a form of fluency practice, since they help the learner to store language as memorised chunks, which are more speedily and more easily accessed than grammar rules. There is a limit, however, to how many chunks a learner can memorise. Perhaps drills should be reserved for high-frequency and formulaic items such as functional language (*Would you like...? How about...?*) and conversational routines (*Did you have a nice weekend? Speak to you later* etc).

The A-factor: Learners who come from educational backgrounds where rote learning and repetition are common practice will feel comfortable with drilling. On the other hand, others may associate drilling with the infant schoolroom, and consider it out of place in an adult learning context. Certainly, when drilling is done to excess, and in the absence of other, more communicative kinds of practice, tedium can set in, cancelling out any of the likely gains.

Sample lesson

Lesson 2: Practising the third conditional using written exercises (Upper intermediate)

The so-called third conditional (*If I had known you were coming, I would have baked a cake*) is typically taught at a relatively advanced stage, both because of its syntactic complexity and because it expresses a concept that is itself fairly opaque, i.e. hypothetical past time. It is not a structure that is easily picked up simply through exposure, and is probably best learned through the conscious study and application of rules. In this example, the teacher has chosen to focus attention on it through a series of written exercises.

Step 1

The teacher distributes cards to different students, on which are written the following words: STUDIED, PASSED, HAVE, HAD, IF, HE, JACK, WOULD, and asks them to stick them on the board to form a sentence, e.g.

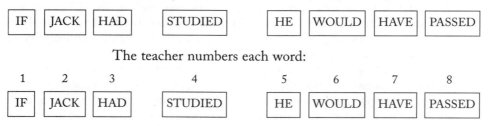

| IF | JACK | HAD | STUDIED | HE | WOULD | HAVE | PASSED |

The teacher numbers each word:

1	2	3	4	5	6	7	8
IF	JACK	HAD	STUDIED	HE	WOULD	HAVE	PASSED

The teacher then distributes further word cards, and invites students to place them in the appropriate column (1–8). For example, JILL, HADN'T, WORKED, FAILED, SHE, WOULDN'T, BOB, DRIVEN SLOWLY, HAD AN ACCIDENT, MARIA, TAKEN A TAXI, BEEN LATE. This results in a table that looks something like this:

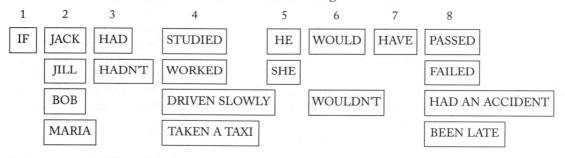

1	2	3	4	5	6	7	8
IF	JACK	HAD	STUDIED	HE	WOULD	HAVE	PASSED
	JILL	HADN'T	WORKED	SHE			FAILED
	BOB		DRIVEN SLOWLY		WOULDN'T		HAD AN ACCIDENT
	MARIA		TAKEN A TAXI				BEEN LATE

Step 2

The teacher then asks students to use the table to write as many sentences as they can, working in pairs. Sample sentences include:

> If Jill hadn't studied, she would have failed.
> If Bob had driven slowly, he wouldn't have had an accident.
> If Maria had taken a taxi, she wouldn't have been late.
> If Maria hadn't driven slowly, she wouldn't have been late.
> If Jack had worked, he wouldn't have had an accident.

Students read out their sentences and the teacher checks them for accuracy, as well as eliminating illogical sentences.

Step 3

The teacher dictates the following situation and asks learners to choose a sentence from the table that completes it:

> Jack had an exam last week. He didn't study for the exam, so he didn't pass. If ...

Possible completions are *If Jack had studied, he would have passed* or ... *he wouldn't have failed.*

The teacher then asks the learners, still working in their pairs, to choose four of their sentences (from Step 2) and write a situation for each sentence, ending in an incomplete *If ...* sentence, as in the teacher's example in Step 3. Having written their situations, they then exchange them with another pair, and complete the *If ...* sentence that each situation generates. They return the sentences for checking.

Step 4

The teacher then hands out a worksheet of situations for which students, working in pairs, devise new sentences using the third conditional. For example:

1 Alex and Anna decided to go to a restaurant. They didn't book a table. When they arrived the restaurant was full and they didn't get a table. *If ...*

2 Chris went for a walk. He didn't take an umbrella. It started raining and he got wet. *If ...*

3 Lisa had a lottery ticket, number 2378. But she lost it. Ticket number 2378 won. The winning prize was a trip to Paris. *If ...*

Discussion

The teacher has adopted an approach to grammar practice that is more thoughtful than the drill-type practice of Sample lesson 1. It is an approach based on the view that accuracy requires an element of reflection. Reflection, in turn, requires time and attention, and is therefore perhaps better mediated through written, rather than spoken, exercises. The challenge to the teacher is to make these written exercises involving, interesting, and collaborative.

So, in Step 1 class attention is focused on the correct ordering of elements in the sentence – that is, how words are 'chained' together. Attention is also directed to the 'slots' in these chains – the words that can substitute for other words in the chain (see Chapter 1, page 2). Together, these chains and slots make up the horizontal and vertical elements of a **substitution table**, which acts as a kind of sentence generator (Step 2). So far, however, the focus has been almost entirely on form, and there is no guarantee that learners understand the concepts underlying the sentences they have generated. It is therefore important to attach meaning to these sentences, hence Step 3, which compels learners to provide a mini-context for their sentences, testing their own understanding of the structure as well as allowing them to test each other. (In monolingual classes it would also be possible to elicit a mother-tongue translation of the sentences they come up with.) So far, the practice has been very controlled in terms of language. Step 4 allows learners a little more freedom, although they are still limited to the form of the third conditional. A natural follow-on to Step 4 might be some form of **personalisation**, where they are encouraged to write true sentences about themselves, but using the third conditional.

Evaluation

The E-factor: In terms of **ease**, written exercises obviously involve more preparation than, say, spoken drills, especially if they are reinforced with card-sorting activities such as in Step 1. However, most ELT coursebooks now come accompanied by workbooks for homework use, and there are a number of self-study grammar books on the market (see, for example, page 44). While these are largely designed for individual use outside the classroom, there is no reason why they shouldn't be exploited for the kind of reflective, collaborative grammar practice work described above. Apart from anything, a phase of low-intensity, book-centred study can provide a welcome change of focus in activity-rich, communicative classrooms. Moreover, written exercises are probably as economical, if not more so, than oral drills, because time spent thinking about language may have important effects on restructuring. It is important, however, that the exercise challenges learners to engage with both form and meaning, and unless there is some kind of problem-solving element, its value in terms of the economical use of classroom time will be reduced. On balance, however, written exercises are probably more effective than drills for targeting accuracy and restructuring.

The A-factor: Most learners, whatever their learning background or preferred learning style, appreciate an opportunity to familarise themselves with a new item by means of unhurried written work. Some may prefer to do this collaboratively, others individually. Allowance should also be made for the learner who may see this kind of activity as being intellectually quite demanding, especially when dealing with concepts such as hypothetical meaning. Nevertheless, there is no reason why relatively simple structures cannot be dealt with in the same way.

Sample lesson

Lesson 3: Practising *can* using an information gap activity (Elementary)

In the following activity, the teacher uses an information gap task in order to target fluency by directing attention to meaning and interaction.

Step 1

The teacher explains the situation: 'You are street musicians. You dance, you sing, and you play an instrument. Your partner has left to join a circus. So you are looking for a new partner – someone who can do the same things as you.'

Step 2

The teacher draws the following grid on the board:

play	sing	dance

She elicits from the class the names of three kinds of musical instrument, three types of singing, and three dances. As students suggest ideas she writes these into the grid (adding *the* if necessary). For example:

play	sing	dance
the violin	opera	the tango
the saxophone	the blues	the cha-cha
the guitar	folk	the waltz

The teacher then asks the students to each choose from the grid one instrument, one singing-type, and one dance. This is 'their street musician's act'. For example, they might choose *the guitar*, *opera*, and *the cha-cha*. Students are instructed to keep their choices 'secret'.

Step 3

The teacher writes this formula on the board: *Can you...?* and elicits possible questions. For example: *Can you play the saxophone? Can you sing the blues? Can you dance the cha-cha?* Students are told that they have to now try and find their new partner, by asking as many other students at least three questions until they find someone who has chosen the same 'combination' as they have. The students then stand up and move around asking their questions. Once they are into the activity, the teacher rubs *Can you ...?* off the board.

Discussion

The activity, although tightly controlled in terms of the language content, ranks as an information gap activity since each student has different 'information': in order to complete the task, they must match their information with that of other students, using language to bridge the gap. There is a communicative purpose to the task, i.e. to find their partner. This means that they not only have to speak but to listen. For it to work, students need to be carefully briefed as to the kind of interaction required, and the language they will need. Thus, the teacher uses an imaginary situation (Step 1) and involves the students in selecting the vocabulary (Step 2). The only 'new' language (*Can you...?*) is provided for them and this provides the scaffolding within which learners can get used to the structure (Step 3). When the activity is well underway, the teacher rubs the 'new' language off the board.

Evaluation

The E-factor: This game type of information gap is extremely **easy** to set up, and the grid idea can be adapted to other situations and structures. For example, to practise *going to*, the teacher can elicit the names of three holiday destinations (e.g. *Acapulco*), three holiday months (e.g. *August*), and three hotel names (e.g. *The Grand*). Students each choose a combination and then question one another in order to find someone going to the same place, in the same month, and staying at the same hotel. Other kinds of information gap exercises involve more preparation, such as the use of pictures (e.g. where students in pairs spot the difference between two pictures) or the use of texts (where, for example, students in pairs have different data, and they have to pool data to complete a task, such as planning a day's outing). Such activities also require careful setting up so that students get the idea that the information which each student has is different.

In terms of **economy** a task like the street musician game is likely to generate a lot of instances of the target language. This is particularly the case if it involves interacting with lots of different students. In pairs, the activity would not work as well, unless the number of choices in each column of the grid were extended from three to, say, ten.

As for **efficacy**, it is debatable the extent to which information gap activities like the one above replicate real-life communication. Obviously, the situation is very contrived, and the language extremely controlled. But as a practice activity this may not be a bad thing. It means that not too many demands are being made on students in terms of their attention. There is a meaning-focus, since they have to listen to each other in order to do the task, and this directs attention away from form. They are free to do this because the form is unvarying and available on the board if they need it. At the same time, the meanings they are expressing are not complicated, so they can also focus on form when they need to. All this should enhance fluency. If it seems too controlled, learners could be asked to supply their own vocabulary rather than use the words in the grid.

Despite the management problems that can arise, the interactive and problem-solving nature of information gap activities put them in another league altogether when compared to drills. They provide a useful intermediate stage in a progression from controlled to freer practice.

The A-factor: However convinced the teacher may be in the usefulness of information gap activities, many students remain sceptical, and are often mystified by the complicated logistics involved in what seems to be nothing more than another grammar exercise. This means that teachers may need to approach this kind of activity cautiously, perhaps briefing students beforehand on the rationale underlying it. A further problem, immediately obvious to teachers of large classes of young learners, is that any activity that involves students milling around may simply be impossible, either because of lack of sufficient space, or because the noise generated would be intolerable. In such a situation, it still may be possible to design the task for groups of a maximum of four or five students.

Sample lesson

Lesson 4: Practising the present perfect using a personalisation task (Elementary)

One weakness of the preceding activity was its lack of **depth**. Learners did not really have to engage, either intellectually or emotionally, with the content of the task. The following activity attempts to meet the conditions for fluency (e.g. a high turnover of chunk-type language) while incorporating an element of personalisation. In this way it aims for a deeper level of personal investment in the task.

Step 1
The teacher writes the following table on the board:

| One person Two people Three people Everyone No one | in our group | has have | + -ed |

He provides an example sentence. For example: *Two people in our group have acted in a play.* He establishes that the time frame implied is that of 'your whole life up to now'. He elicits other verbs that could fill the fourth column of the table, including a range of common irregular verbs such as *seen, been to, had, met, eaten, done, gone* etc.

Step 2
The teacher puts the class into groups of four, with the instruction that they should produce as many true sentences about their group as they can in ten minutes, using only sentences generated by the table. A spokesperson is appointed for each group who will have the job of reporting on some of the more interesting findings. The teacher monitors the group work, checking that students are on task, and providing help with vocabulary when needed.

Step 3
The teacher brings the class back to 'plenary' mode, and asks the spokesperson from each group to report on some of the more interesting sentences. In the case of sentences beginning *One person ...* or *Two/Three people ...* he invites the other students to guess who is being referred to. He also asks some students to elaborate on their experiences, by asking questions such as *When did that happen? How did you feel at the time?* etc.

Step 4
Individually students write sentences about people in their class, based on the preceding activity. For example:

Tatyana has been to Australia.
Elena has eaten ostrich meat.
Yevgeni has worked in a restaurant.

Discussion
The activity has many of the features of a traditional pattern practice drill in that the structure is tightly controlled and there is a high degree of repetition of the basic pattern. The difference is that the content of the drill is provided by the students themselves, working from the model provided in the form of a substitution table (Step 1). Moreover, because the students are working in groups (Step 2) the activity is both more student-centred and

more meaning-focused: there is less emphasis on accuracy at this stage. The pressure to be accurate comes in Step 3, when students are reporting their group's sentences. (It would be a good idea, therefore, to select as spokespeople those students who might normally pay less attention to form.) Again, a focus on accuracy is provided in Step 4, where, by being asked to write sentences, students' attention is brought back to form, where previously it had been more concerned with the meaning. This stage also provides them with a useful record of the lesson, made more memorable through having been personalised.

Evaluation

The E-factor: The activity is extremely **easy** to set up: all that is needed is a board, and once students are familiar with the activity-type, not even that. Note also that the activity can be adapted to virtually any grammatical structure. For example:

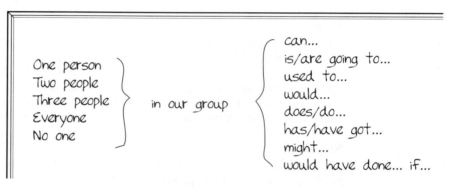

Moreover, the activity rates highly in terms of **economy**, since the minimal setting up has excellent pay-off in terms of the volume of practice generated. Theoretically, there is no limit to the number of sentences the groups could produce.

As for **efficacy**, the activity meets a number of the conditions for effective fluency activities outlined above. The language is fairly formulaic and there is a high volume of repetition of the formulae; a secure scaffold is provided in the form of the table, but form is de-emphasised since learners' main concern is to create meaningful sentences. Moreover, the activity works just as well with classes of mixed ability, in that learners can contribute to the level of their ability.

Finally, in terms of forging a group dynamic, the activity has positive spin-off, since students are obliged to interact and find out things about each other they might not otherwise have known. Note that to do this they will need to be familiar with the question forms, such as *Have you ever ...?* and *Who has/hasn't ...?* It would pay to write these on the board in advance of the group work.

The A-factor: Some students – because of their educational or cultural background, or due to personality factors – might find personalisation tasks threatening or out of place in the language classroom. There is also the problem that learners may feel such pressure to be 'interesting' that they become anxious, and lose sight of the linguistic purpose of the task. It may help if learners were given the option of 'passing' when topics come up that they do not wish to commit themselves to.

Sample lesson

Lesson 5: Practising the passive using a grammar interpretation activity (Elementary)

Typically grammar practice involves language **production**, that is, either writing or speaking. This derives from the belief that the sooner learners start producing accurate language, the better. An alternative view is that learners first need to engage with new language **receptively** – that is through listening and reading. Advocates of this position argue for the importance of what is called **consciousness-raising** as a means of restructuring the learner's grammar. Accordingly, a number of researchers have devised exercise types called either **grammar interpretation activities** or **structured-input tasks**. Such tasks require learners to process input which has been specially structured so as to help them understand the target item. There is no immediate need to produce the item. In fact, immediate production may be counterproductive, in that it may distract attention away from the brain work involved in understanding and restructuring.

In the following example, the teacher has chosen a grammar interpretation activity to sensitise a group of elementary students to the difference between active and passive verb forms.

Step 1

The teacher distributes the pictures (A–J) on the following page – or alternatively, displays them on the board using an overhead projector.

She then tells the class to listen to the sentences she is going to read, and to match each sentence with its picture. She reads each of the following sentences aloud – along with its number – repeating them if students seem confused.

1   The man hit the bus.
2   The man was hit by the bus.
3   The Queen was driven to the airport.
4   The old woman attacked a policeman.
5   The dog followed a cat.
6   The clown chased the lion.
7   The old woman was attacked by a policeman.
8   The dog was followed by a cat.
9   The Queen drove to the airport.
10   The clown was chased by a lion.

Step 2

After allowing students to compare their answers with a partner, the teacher then distributes the written sentences, or writes them on the board. Students check their answers again, before the teacher checks the task with the class.

Step 3

The teacher asks the students to turn the written sentences over (or she rubs them off the board). In pairs, the students use the pictures to reconstruct the sentences from memory, writing two sentences for each of these prompts:

The man ...
The Queen ...
The old woman ...
The dog ...
The clown ...

Students read their sentences aloud for checking, or compare them with the sentences on their handout.

Discussion

The activity is called a **grammar interpretation** activity because, in order to do the matching task, learners have to 'interpret' the difference between active and passive forms. For those students still unfamiliar with the difference the exercise **problematises** the language point, forcing them to acknowledge the effect of making one grammatical choice over another. Note that the exercise (until Step 3) is **receptive**: unlike traditional grammar practice exercises, the student does not have to supply the targeted language item.

Evaluation

The E-factor: Since most published grammar practice activities are production-based, teachers who want to incorporate grammar interpretation exercises into their teaching are going to have to design many of them themselves, a factor that detracts from their **easiness**. Nevertheless, many production exercises can be turned into comprehension exercises. The following exercise is easily adapted:

> Write sentences with the present perfect continuous for these situations:
> 1 Ben started work five hours ago. He is still working.
> 2 Rebecca joined the queue for tickets 30 minutes ago. She is still queuing.

Here is the exercise turned into a comprehension activity:

> Choose the best summary of each situation:
> 1 Ben started work five hours ago. He is still working.
>   a Ben is working for five hours.
>   b Ben was working for five hours.
>   c Ben has been working for five hours.
> 2 Rebecca joined the queue for tickets 30 minutes ago. She bought her ticket 10 minutes ago.
>   a Rebecca is queuing for 20 minutes.
>   b Rebecca was queuing for 20 minutes.
>   c Rebecca has been queuing for 20 minutes.

Notice that these tasks work only when two (or more) similar forms are being contrasted.

Grammar interpretation tasks are an **economical** way of drawing learners' attention to grammatical choices: they require minimal means to make major distinctions. As for **efficacy**, their power to prompt students to notice features of the input and hence to raise consciousness suggests that they rate highly. If nothing else, such tasks are likely to have a beneficial effect on reading and listening skills. Also, the fact that learners work collaboratively on the task increases the chance of peer-teaching.

The A-factor: Grammar-interpretation tasks will appeal to students who enjoy problem-solving activities, but those who don't may feel frustrated. In this sense, they share many of the characteristics of inductive grammar presentations (see Chapter 4). Nevertheless, there are many students who may find immediate production of new language – in the form, for example, of drills – off-putting, even threatening, and who would therefore welcome the chance to 'get their minds around' new language in advance of 'getting their tongues around' it.

Sample lesson

Lesson 6: Practising *going to* using conversation (Elementary)

Conversation – or chat – between teacher and students, if it takes place at all, is customarily confined to the beginnings and endings of lessons. Yet there are grounds to suppose that conversation provides a rich language environment for integrating new language. Experienced teachers will know that it is possible to have conversations with learners of even quite low levels, simply by asking *yes/no* questions, and by prompting, and if necessary, reformulating the learners' answers. In this way, conversations provide the ideal **scaffolding** within which learners can take risks in the knowledge that, if they trip up, there will be someone to help them. As speakers become more proficient, these verbal scaffolds can be gradually dismantled.

In the following example, the teacher of a class of elementary teenage students is using a conversation to embed examples of *going to* to talk about future plans.

Step 1

The teacher seats the students in a circle, occupying one seat in the circle himself. He then initiates a conversation about the weekend along these lines:

TEACHER: So, Fransesc, what are you going to do this weekend? What are your plans?

FRANSESC: I study.

1 → TEACHER: You're going to study, are you? What are you going to study?

FRANSESC: Mathematics.

TEACHER: Why mathematics?

FRANSESC: Have an exam.

	TEACHER:	You've got an exam? What, next week?
	FRANSESC:	Yes. I have.
	TEACHER:	So you're going to stay at home and study?
	FRANSESC:	Yes. I going to study.
	TEACHER:	And what about you, Carla? What are you going to do?
	CARLA:	On Saturday I go to shopping.
2 →	TEACHER:	On Saturday, you're going to go shopping?
	CARLA:	Yes.
	TEACHER:	Again.
	CARLA:	On Saturday I going to go shopping.
3 →	TEACHER:	'I'm going'.
	CARLA:	I'm going to go shopping.
	TEACHER:	What are you going to buy?
	CARLA:	I going to buy *no sé* [I don't know] maybe a new jeans ...
	TEACHER:	You're going to buy new jeans. And in the evening?
	CARLA:	I go to party ...
	TEACHER:	You're going to a party? What are you going to wear? Your new ...?
	CARLA:	Yes, maybe I'm wear a new jeans.
4 →	TEACHER:	'I'm going to wear my new jeans.' Again.
	CARLA:	I'm going to wear a new jeans.
	TEACHER:	And Ramón, what are you going to do ...?

Step 2

The conversation continues in this vein until most students have been involved. Then the teacher says:

	TEACHER:	And me? What about me? [pause]
	CARMEN:	What about you?
	TEACHER:	What ...?
	CARMEN:	What will you do this weekend?
	TEACHER:	What am I going to do?
	CARMEN:	Yes. What you are going to do?
	TEACHER:	'What are you going to do?'
	CARMEN:	What are you going to do?
	TEACHER:	I'm going to buy a table. [pause]
	RAUL:	What a what kind a table?
	TEACHER:	A dining table.
	FRANSESC:	*¿Qué?* [What?]
	TEACHER:	A dining table. A table for eating, you know. [gestures]
	RAUL:	Why?
5 →	TEACHER:	Why am I going to buy a dining table? Because I don't have one!
	RAMÓN:	How are you ... where are you eat your ...?
	CARLA:	Where you are going to buy a table?
	TEACHER:	I don't know. Any ideas?

Step 3

When the teacher decides that the conversation has run its course, he goes to the board and elicits some questions and answers using *going to* which he writes on the board. For example:

What are you going to do this weekend?   I'm going to study.

What are you going to wear?   I'm going to wear my new jeans.

Where are you going to buy your table?   I'm going to buy it in town.

Step 4

He then asks students, in pairs, to have a similar conversation about the following week. He monitors this, correcting and providing vocabulary where necessary.

Step 5

The teacher sets a writing task for homework, which is to write ten sentences about their plans for the weekend and the following week.

Discussion

For conversation to work in the classroom, a number of conditions need to apply, one of the most important being the teacher's genuine interest in the students as people. But a genuine interest in itself is not sufficient unless it is reflected in the teacher's behaviour, including such things as manner, voice, body language, eye-contact, and use of names. The way the class is organised is very important as well (Step 1), and even if students cannot sit in a circle, it is imperative that they can all see and hear each other, and that the teacher is seated too. The teacher's role is to provide a verbal scaffold within which the learners can feel safe. At the same time, he uses the conversational structure as a means to introduce and reinforce the targeted language item: this, after all, is not real conversation; rather it is an **instructional conversation**, because it is taking place in a classroom. Nevertheless, the teacher is able to maintain the focus on the meanings that he and the students are jointly constructing, while at the same time nudging students to pay some attention to the form of *going to*. For example, he **reformulates** students' utterances (as in the turns marked 1 and 2, for example); he **extends** students' utterances (turn 5); and he even explicitly **corrects** some utterances (turns 3 and 4, for example). What's more, he manages the interaction in such a way that, as well as asking questions of the students, the students are directed to ask him questions (Step 2). In this way the structure gets thoroughly manipulated, and, at the same time, the conversation achieves a more natural symmetry. In Step 4, the focus shifts away from the teacher-student interaction, to a student-student one, thereby increasing the amount of speaking time all round, while allowing the teacher to monitor the extent to which learners are accurately and appropriately incorporating the target structure. As a final insurance that the form of *going to* isn't sacrificed to conversational fluency, the homework task (Step 5) serves as a kind of student-generated drill-type activity, and a useful summary of the lesson.

Evaluation

The E-factor: Nothing is **easier** (nor is anything more difficult if you are not used to it) than simply talking to students. It requires no preparation, no technology (although recording the conversation 'live' provides an excellent resource for further language work) and it is feasible even with classes of 20 students or more. It is less **economical**, in terms of how much each student can potentially contribute, than small group work, but, as in the example above, it can act as a useful preparatory stage for group or pair work. Not all structures are equally easy to incorporate with a notice-ably high frequency into a single conversation: in fact, to do so might make the conversation stilted and heavy going. Nevertheless, high frequency grammar items, such as the present simple, past simple, and modal verbs such as *should*, *would*, *could* and *might* are fairly easily and naturally con-textualised in informal chat.

In terms of its **efficacy**, there has been little research into how well instructional conversation works for second language learning. Never-theless, there is considerable anecdotal evidence from language learners in non-classroom settings who have reached high levels of proficiency solely through interacting in conversational contexts.

The A-factor: For students who expect the teacher to maintain the role of lecturer, including the social distance that such a role assumes, free-ranging and informal conversation will baffle them, and, especially if the class is a large one, may prove impossible. Obviously, the smaller the group, the better the chance of all students participating, but a lot also depends on the group dynamic that has been created. However, conversation can itself improve a dynamic that may be sluggish, especially if combined with the judicious use of personalisation activities (see Sample lesson 4 above).

Conclusions

In this chapter we have looked at ways that grammatical knowledge is automised through practice. Practice activities are conventionally aimed at improving both accuracy and fluency of production. They can also provide conditions for increasing the complexity of the learner's developing language system – a process also known as restructuring. Practice activities need not be aimed solely at production, but, as in the case of grammar interpretation tasks, can serve to develop the receptive processing of grammar as well.

A number of key criteria for choosing, designing and evaluating practice activities have been mentioned. Perhaps they can be reduced to essentially two factors:

- The **quantity** factor: simply put, this means the more practice the better. But quantity of practice is not enough unless the practice meets the following condition:
- The **quality** factor: practice needs to juggle attention to form in the interests of accuracy, with attention to meaning in the interests of fluency.

Looking ahead   Practice may – in the long term – make perfect, but on the way the learner is inevitably going to produce language that falls short of the target, in terms of its intelligibility or appropriacy, or both. How the teacher deals with flawed output will have an important bearing on the learner's chances of ultimate success, and is the focus of the next chapter.

7 How to deal with grammar errors

- **What are errors?**
- **Attitudes to error and correction**
- **Responding to errors**
- **Sample lesson 1: Using learners' errors to review cohesive devices**
- **Sample lesson 2: Teaching grammar through reformulation**

What are errors? Language learners make mistakes. This seems to happen regardless of the teacher's skill and perseverance. It seems to be an inevitable part of learning a language. Most teachers believe that to ignore these mistakes might put at risk the learner's linguistic development. Current research tends to support this view. Not to ignore mistakes, however, often means having to make a number of on-the-spot decisions. These can be summed up in the form of the 'in-flight' questions a teacher might ask when faced with a student's possible error:

- Is there an error here?
- What kind of error is it?
- What caused it?
- Does it matter?
- What should I do about it?

Here, for example, is a written text produced by a Spanish-speaking student:

> The Sunday night past, the doorbell rangs, I opened the door and I had a big surprise, my brother was stopping in the door. He was changing a lot of. He was having a long hair but him looking was very interesting. Now, he's twenty five years, and he's lower. We speaked all night and we remembered a lot of thinks. At last when I went to the bed was the four o'clock.

While it is clear that the text is non-standard (by native-speaker standards) it is not always an easy task to identify the individual errors themselves. Take for example, *I had a big surprise*. At first sight there seems to be nothing wrong with this. It is a grammatically well-formed sentence – that is, the words are in the right order, the tense is correct, and the subject and verb agree. Moreover, the meaning is clear and unambiguous. But would a native speaker ever say it? According to **corpus** evidence (that is, databases of spoken and written texts) something can *be a big surprise*, a person can *be*

113

in for a big surprise, you can *have a big surprise for someone*, but instances of *I had a big surprise* simply do not exist. Should we conclude, therefore, that it is wrong? The answer is yes, if we imagine a scale of 'wrongness' ranging from 'completely wrong' to 'this is OK, but a native speaker would never say it'. However, no corpus is big enough to include all possible sentences and, at the same time, new ways of saying things are being constantly invented. This is a case, therefore, when the teacher has to use considerable discretion.

Once an error has been identified, the next step is to classify it. Learners may make mistakes at the level of individual words, in the way they put sentences together, or at the level of whole texts. At the word level, learners make mistakes either because they have chosen the wrong word for the meaning they want to express (*My brother was stopping in the door* instead of *standing*), or they have chosen the wrong form of the word (*lower* instead of *lawyer*, *thinks* instead of *things*). These are **lexical errors**. Lexical errors also include mistakes in the way words are combined: *the Sunday night past* instead of *last Sunday night*. **Grammar errors**, on the other hand, cover such things as mistakes in verb form and tense (*the doorbell rangs, we speaked*), and in sentence structure: *was the four o'clock*, where the subject of the clause (*it*) has been left out. There is also a category of errors called **discourse errors** which relate to the way sentences are organised and linked in order to make whole texts. For example, in the student extract above *at last* suggests that what follows is the solution to a problem: *eventually* would have been better in this context.

To sum up, then, the following categories of errors have been identified:

- lexical errors
- grammar errors
- discourse errors

and, in the case of spoken language:

- pronunciation errors

It is not always the case that errors fall neatly into the above categories, and there is often considerable overlap between these categories.

Identifying the cause of an error can be equally problematic. Speakers of Spanish may recognise, in the above text, the influence of the writer's first language (his **L1**) on his second language (his **L2**). For example, the lack of the indefinite article in *he's lower* (for *he's a lawyer*) suggests that the learner has borrowed the Spanish construction (*es abogado*) in which the indefinite article (*un*) is not used. Such instances of L1 influence on L2 production are examples of **transfer**. They do not necessarily result in errors – there is such a thing as **positive transfer**. *He's lower* is an example of **negative transfer** or what was once called L1 **interference**.

The case of *rangs*, however, cannot be accounted for by reference to the learner's L1. Nor can *speaked*. Both errors derive from over-applying (or **overgeneralising**) an L2 rule. In the case of *rangs*, the learner has overgeneralised the third person -*s* rule in the present (*he rings*) and applied it to the past. In the case of *speaked* he has overgeneralised the past tense -*ed* ending. Such errors seem to be influenced not by factors external to the second language such as the learner's first language but by the nature of the second language itself. They suggest that the learner is working according to L2 rules and this is evidence that a process of hypothesis formation and testing is underway. In fact, these **developmental errors** are not dissimilar to the kinds of errors children make when they are learning their mother tongue:

> He go to sleep.
> Are dogs can wiggle their tails?
> Daddy broked it.

These two kinds of errors — transfer and developmental — account for the bulk of the errors learners make. Such errors can range from the fairly hit-and-miss (*him looking was very interesting*) to errors that seem to show evidence of a rule being fairly systematically (but not yet accurately) applied. Thus: *my brother was stopping, he was changing, he was having a long hair.* These are all examples of a verb form (past continuous) being over-used, but in a systematic way. It is as if the learner had formed a rule to the effect that, 'when talking about past states — as opposed to events — use *was + -ing*'.

It is probably these **systematic errors**, rather than the random ones, that respond best to correction. Correction can provide the feedback the learner needs to help confirm or reject a hypothesis, or to tighten the application of a rule that is being applied fairly loosely. Of course, it is not always clear whether an error is the product of random processes, or the product of a developing but inexact system. Nor is it always clear how inexact this system is. For example, it may be the case that the learner knows the right rule but, in the heat of the moment, has failed to apply it. One way of testing this is to see whether the learner can **self-correct**: could the writer of the text above change *speaked* to *spoke*, for example, if told that *speaked* was wrong? If so, this suggests that the rule is both systematic and correctly formulated in the learner's mind, but that it hasn't yet become automatic.

The next issue to address is the question of priorities. Which errors really matter, and which don't? This is obviously rather subjective: some errors are likely to distract or even irritate the reader or listener while others go largely unnoticed. For example, speakers of languages in which nouns are distinguished by gender (e.g. *un banane, une pomme*) frequently say they are irritated by gender mistakes such as *une banane*. A fairer, but still fairly subjective, criterion might be the one of **intelligibility**: to what extent does the error interfere with, or distort, the speaker's (or writer's) message? In the text above it is difficult, even impossible, to recover the meaning of *lower* (for *lawyer*) from the context. On the other hand *the doorbell rangs* is fairly unproblematic. It may cause a momentary hiccup in communication, but it is not severe enough to threaten it.

It should be apparent by now that there are many complex decisions that teachers have to make when monitoring learner production. It is not surprising that the way they respond to error tends to be more often intuitive than consciously considered. But before addressing the question as to how to respond, it may pay to look briefly at teachers' and students' attitudes to error and correction.

Attitudes to error and correction

Few people like being wrong, and yet there seems to be no way of learning a language without being wrong a lot of the time. Not many people like being corrected either, yet to leave mistakes uncorrected flies in the face of the intuitions and expectations of teachers and students alike. This accounts for some of the problems associated with error and correction.

Attitudes to error run deep and lie at the heart of teachers' intuitions about language learning. Many people still believe that errors are contagious, and that learners are at risk of catching the errors other learners make. It is often this fear of error infection that underlies many students' dislike of pair and group work. On the other hand, many teachers believe that to correct errors is a form of interference, especially in fluency activities. Some teachers go further, and argue that correction of any sort creates a judgmental – and therefore stressful – classroom atmosphere, and should be avoided altogether.

These different attitudes find an echo in the shifts of thinking that have taken place amongst researchers and materials writers. Recent thinking sees errors as being evidence of developmental processes rather than the result of bad habit formation. This sea change in attitudes is well captured in the introductions to ELT coursebooks. Here is a selection:

'The student should be trained to learn by making as few mistakes as possible ... He must be trained to adopt correct learning habits right from the start.'
(from *First Things First* by L. Alexander)

'Getting things wrong is only good practice in getting things wrong.'
(from *Success with English, Teacher's Handbook 1* by Barnett et al)

'Provided students communicate effectively, they should not be given a sense of failure because they make mistakes.'
(from *The Cambridge English Course, 1, Teacher's Book* by Swan and Walter)

'Don't expect learners to go straight from ignorance to knowledge. Learning takes time and is not achieved in one go. Be prepared to accept partial learning as an important stage on the way to full learning.'
(from *Project English 2, Teacher's Book* by Hutchinson)

'Making mistakes is an important and positive part of learning a language. Only by experimenting with the language and receiving feedback can students begin to work out how the language works.'
(from *Blueprint Intermediate, Teacher's Book* by Abbs and Freebairn)

Certainly, current methodology is much more tolerant of error. But the tide may be turning yet again. Studies of learners whose language development has **fossilised** – that is, it has stopped at a point well short of the target –

suggest that lack of **negative feedback** may have been a factor. Negative feedback is simply indicating *No, you can't say that* when a learner makes an error. Positive feedback, on the other hand, is when learners are told when they are right. If the only messages learners get are positive, it may be the case that there is no incentive to restructure their mental grammar. The restructuring mechanisms close down. Hence it is now generally accepted that a **focus on form** (not just on meaning) is necessary in order to guard against fossilisation. A focus on form includes giving learners clear messages about their errors.

Responding to errors

What options has the teacher got when faced with a student's error? Let's imagine that, in the course of a classroom activity, a student has been describing a person's appearance and said:

He has a long hair.

Here are some possible responses that the teacher might consider:

1 *No.* This is clearly negative feedback, but it offers the student no clue as to what was wrong. The teacher may be assuming that the student has simply made a slip under pressure, and that this does not therefore represent a lack of knowledge of the rule. The learner should therefore be able to self-correct. There are, of course, other ways of signalling that a mistake has been made without having to say *No.* A facial expression, shake of the head etc, might work just as well. Some teachers try to soften the negative force of *no* by, for example, making a *mmmm* noise to indicate: *Well, that's not entirely correct but thanks anyway.* Unfortunately, this may leave the student wondering *Have I made a mistake or haven't I?*

2 *He has long hair.* This a correction in the strictest sense of the word. The teacher simply repairs the student's utterance – perhaps in the interest of maintaining the flow of the talk, but at the same time, reminding the learner not to focus only on meaning at the expense of form.

3 *No article.* The teacher's move is directed at pinpointing the kind of error the student has made in order to prompt self-correction, or, if that fails, **peer-correction** – when learners correct each other. This is where **metalanguage** (the use of grammatical terminology) comes in handy: words like *article*, *preposition*, *verb*, *tense* etc. provide an economical means of giving feedback – assuming, of course, that students are already familiar with these terms.

4 *No. Anyone?* An unambiguous feedback signal plus an invitation for peer-correction. By excluding the option of self-correction, however, the teacher risks humiliating the original student: perhaps the teacher knows the student well enough to rule out self-correction for this error.

5 *He has ...?* In other words, the teacher is replaying the student's utterance up to the point where the error occurred, with a view to isolating

the error as a clue for self-correction. This technique can be reinforced by **finger-coding**, where the teacher marks out each word on her fingers, indicating with her fingers the part of the phrase or sentence that needs repair.

6 *He has a long hair?* Another common teacher strategy is to echo the mistake but with a quizzical intonation. This is perhaps less threatening than saying *No*, but often learners fail to interpret this is an invitation to self-correct, and think that the teacher is simply questioning the truth of what they have just said. They might then respond *Yes, he has a very long hair. Down to here.*

7 *I'm sorry, I didn't understand.* Variations on this response include *Sorry? He what? Excuse me?* etc. These are known as **clarification requests** and, of course, occur frequently in real conversation. As a correction device they signal to the student that the meaning of their message is unclear, suggesting that it may have been distorted due to some problem of form. It is therefore a more friendly way of signalling a mistake. Research suggests that when learners re-cast their message after receiving a clarification request, it usually tends to improve, despite their not having been told explicitly that a mistake has been made, much less what kind of mistake it was. This suggests that the policy of 'acting a bit thick' (on the part of the teacher) might have positive dividends in terms of self-correction.

8 *Just one? Like this?* [draws bald man with one long hair] *Ha ha ...* The teacher has pretended to interpret the student's utterance literally, in order to show the student the unintended effect of the error, on the principle that, once the student appreciates the difference between *he has long hair* and *he has a long hair* he will be less likely to make the same mistake again. This is possible only with those mistakes which do make a difference in meaning – such as *he's lower* in the text we started with. There is, of course, the danger of humiliating the student, but, if handled sensitively, this kind of feedback can be extremely effective.

9 *A long hair is just one single hair, like you find in your soup. For the hair on your head you wouldn't use an article: He has long hair.* The teacher uses the error to make an impromptu teaching point. This is an example of **reactive** teaching, where instruction is in response to students' errors rather than trying to pre-empt them. Of course, if the teacher were to do this at every mistake, the classes would not only become very teacher-centred, but the students might become reluctant to open their mouths.

10 *Oh, he has long hair, has he?* This technique (sometimes called **reformulation**) is an example of covert feedback, disguised as a conversational aside. The hope is, that the student will take the veiled correction on board but will not be inhibited from continuing the flow of talk. Typically, this is the way parents seem to correct their children – by offering an expanded version of the child's utterance:

CHILD: Teddy hat.
MOTHER: Yes, Teddy's got a hat on, hasn't he?

Some theorists argue that these expansions and reformulations help provide a temporary **scaffold** for the child's developing language competence. The problem is that learners may simply not recognise the intention nor notice the difference between their utterance and the teacher's reformulation.

11 *Good*. Strange as this seems, it is in fact a very common way that teachers provide feedback on student production, especially in activities where the focus is more on meaning than on form. For example, it is not difficult to imagine a sequence like this:

TEACHER: What does Mick Jagger look like?
STUDENT: He has a long hair.
TEACHER: Good. Anything else?
STUDENT: He has a big lips.
TEACHER: Good.
etc.

The intention behind *good* (or any of its alternatives, such as *OK*) is to acknowledge the students' contribution, irrespective of either its accuracy or even of its meaning. But, if construed as positive feedback, it may lull learners into a false sense of security, and, worse, initiate the process of fossilisation.

12 Teacher says nothing but writes down error for future reference. The intention here is to postpone the feedback so as not to disrupt the flow of talk, but to deal with errors later. Perhaps the students are working in groups and the teacher has chanced on the error while monitoring. A correction in this context might be inappropriate. Nevertheless, there are some grounds to believe that the most effective feedback is that which occurs in what are called **real operating conditions**, that is, when the learner is using language communicatively. For example, a trainee driver is more likely to notice the correction when it is most relevant – while driving – than after the event, in a list of points being ticked off by the driving instructor. The trick, it seems, is to intervene without interfering.

To sum up, then: learners' errors offer the teacher a rich source of data with which to monitor learning. At the same time, learners need feedback on their production. This suggests that teachers should deal with at least some of the errors that arise. To do this, they have a wide range of feedback options available. The choice of feedback strategy will depend on such factors as:

- The type of error: Does it have a major effect on communication? Is it one that the learner could probably self-repair?
- The type of activity: Is the focus of the activity more on form or on meaning? If the latter, it is probably best to correct without interfering too much with the flow of communication.

- The type of learner: Will the learner be discouraged or humiliated by correction? Alternatively, will the learner feel short-changed if there is *no* correction?

Sample lesson

Lesson 1: Using learners' errors to review cohesive devices (Intermediate)

In this lesson the teacher (in a class of mixed nationalities in Australia) is using a sampling of learners' errors to highlight a feature of cohesion – that is, the way sentences and parts of sentences are connected by words like *and*, *but*, *however*, and *so* etc.

Step 1

The teacher hands out a worksheet which consists of a number of sentences she has collected from their previous written work. (These sentences could also be presented on the board or by means of an overhead projector.) She asks the students first of all to attempt to correct them, working in pairs, and then to identify one feature they all have in common. This is the worksheet:

---

1 I have no girlfriend in spite handsome boy.

2 The Little Red Riding Hood has dropped into the forest nevertheless her mother's warning.

3 I eat chocolate everyday inspite I have to do diet.

4 I came to Australia nevertheless a lot of interesting places is in Japan.

5 I will stay at home this weekend nevertheless my boyfriend will spend his time on the beach.

Step 2

The teacher monitors the pair work, helping learners sort out some of the peripheral problems, for example, the wrong choice of tense or vocabulary, as in *has dropped into* (for which she suggests simply *went*). She deliberately avoids dealing with *despite* and *nevertheless* at this stage, but instead encourages students to try and work out the solution themselves.

Step 3

The teacher then distributes a handout (see the opposite page) which she asks learners to study before returning to the sentence correction task.

> **Contrast**
>
> When contrasting two surprising facts, the most common way is to use *but*:
>
> The film was long but I didn't get bored.
>
> Some other ways of expressing contrast are:
>
> Linking ideas in ONE sentence:
>
> 1 *in spite of* + NOUN   In spite of the film's length, I didn't get bored.
>
> 2 *in spite of the fact that* + CLAUSE   In spite of the fact that the film was long, I didn't get bored.
>
> Linking TWO sentences:
>
> 1 *nevertheless* + sentence   The film was long. Nevertheless, I didn't get bored.

Step 4

The teacher then elicits corrected versions of the sentences in open class, writing these on the board, and drawing attention to the linking devices (*in spite of [the fact that]; nevertheless*) by underlining them, and asking individuals to explain their use. There are obviously several ways of recasting the example sentences; the following are suggested corrections:

> 1 I am a handsome boy. Nevertheless, I don't have a girlfriend.
>
> 2 Little Red Riding Hood went into the forest in spite of her mother's warning.
>
> 3 In spite of the fact that I am on a diet, I eat chocolate every day.
>
> 4 There are a lot of interesting places in Japan. Nevertheless, I came to Australia.
>
> 5 I'm going to stay at home this weekend in spite of the fact that my boyfriend is going to spend it at the beach.

Step 5

The teacher then hands out an exercise which requires the students to make the correct choice of linking device. For example:

Complete these sentences using *in spite of*, *in spite of the fact that*, or *nevertheless*.

1 We went to the beach _____ it was a rather cold day.

2 It was a rather cold day. _____, we went to the beach.

3 _____ the cold, we went to the beach.

Discussion

Teaching students of intermediate level or above inevitably involves a fair amount of review and remedial teaching. The core grammar areas are by now familiar territory, and, apart from vocabulary, there is not a lot of new language left to encounter. The problem is that their 'old' language is neither accurate nor automatic. Fluency practice can target the latter aim, but accuracy may be best dealt with by means of a more reactive, and at the same time, more reflective approach. Simply to present previously studied items all over again may be both time-wasting and demotivating. Using learners' errors for consciousness-raising purposes offers the teacher an alternative to presentation, while at the same time it 'customises' the lesson, tailoring it to the specific problems of the students.

Handing out a worksheet of anonymous errors (Step 1) avoids the problem of targeting (and possibly shaming) individual students. At the same time, the teacher can include errors which she has collected from other groups, thereby enriching her database. In Step 2 the intention is to tidy up the errors before homing in on the targeted language area. (The teacher could, of course, circumvent this stage, by tidying up the errors herself when preparing the worksheet.) By preparing an explanatory handout (Step 3) the teacher maintains the learner-centred focus: only in Step 4 does the teacher assume her traditional role at the board, in order to knit together any loose ends, before handing back to the students again (Step 5) at the testing stage.

Evaluation

The E-factor: Assembling a collection of learners' errors is relatively **easy** where teachers have access to personal computers. It requires only a little extra time, when marking written work, to key in one or two errors per student. More difficult is capturing spoken errors: recording students from time to time can help build up a useful database. It pays to organise the collected errors into categories – tense, modals, vocabulary, word order etc. This will greatly facilitate preparation of future classes. Preparation of grammar handouts (as in the sample lesson) is also time-consuming: the wide range of self-study grammars now available, as well as the grammar reference notes in current coursebooks, now makes the writing of grammar handouts virtually unnecessary.

As a means of directing attention on form, and assuming that the errors have been pre-selected and even tidied up so as to reduce the danger of overload, the use of students' errors is extremely **economical**. There is no area of language, for a start, that can't be approached in this way. Also, authentic errors have a credibility that invented examples seldom have: students often recognise errors – even ones they didn't make themselves. For this reason error analysis of this kind is particularly effective for highlighting L1 transfer mistakes, such as the Spanish speaker's *It's the best film I have never seen*. Students could be encouraged to keep a list of these in their notebooks, or prepare posters for the classroom wall, captioned, for example, Our Favourite Mistakes.

Finally, the fact that the grammar lesson has been planned around the errors the learners have actually made, rather than having been planned to pre-empt the errors they might make, makes considerable sense. It has been argued that a lot of grammar teaching is probably largely redundant, since it is motivated not so much by the problems that learners really have as by the simple fact that the item in question has been described by linguists and grammarians: because it is there, let's teach it. An error-driven approach attempts to redress this tendency, focusing instruction on what really matters, which argues in favour of its **effectiveness**.

The A-factor: There is always the danger that, by emphasising the negative, a focus on the errors they have made may serve to discourage learners. However, students generally react positively to this very direct treatment of their errors, preferring it to more covert approaches. Most students accept that explicit feedback on error is an essential component of classroom learning – the real difference, in fact, between focused instruction and random acquisition. In order to convey a more positive message, however, it pays, from time to time, to intersperse correct sentences (from students' output) amongst the incorrect ones, and ask students first of all to sort them into these two categories.

Sample lesson

Lesson 2: Teaching grammar through reformulation (Elementary)

Reformulation is the process by which the teacher takes the meanings the learners are attempting to express in English and 'translates' these into an acceptable form. It is a technique that has been used in the teaching of writing. Students write a first draft, which the teacher then reformulates, not just at the level of individual words and sentences, but in terms of the organisation of the text as a whole. Reformulation is therefore more than simply correction. Whereas correction is offered in the spirit of *This is how you **should** say it*, the impetus underlying reformulation is more: *This is how I would say it*.

In this lesson the teacher introduces the language used for talking about disasters by reformulating a text jointly constructed by the students.

Step 1

The teacher introduces the theme by placing a newspaper picture of a disaster, such as an earthquake, on the board. He sits and, without giving explicit prompts (such as *What happens in an earthquake?* or *Have you ever been in an earthquake?*) but simply by indicating with a look or gesture that students should say anything they want associated with the topic, he encourages the production of isolated words, phrases and sentences. These are left uncorrected: the focus at this stage is simply on brainstorming ideas.

Step 2
When students are starting to run out of ideas (even with some gentle prompting from the teacher), or when they start departing too widely from the topic, the teacher stops the activity and draws a line down the centre of the board. He hands one student the chalk and asks this student to act as the class scribe. Her job is, working with the whole class, to collate the ideas that the students have produced about the topic, and to write them up on to the board. The teacher then leaves the classroom or sits at the back. The class then collaboratively construct a text which the scribe writes up on to one half of the board.

Step 3
The teacher returns and reads the students' text aloud, without commentary, but asking any questions where the meaning is unclear. He then reformulates this text on to the other half of the board – that is, he rewrites it in its entirety, correcting superficial errors of spelling, word choice, collocation, and morphology, recasting complete sentences if necessary, and even moving whole sentences around so as to produce a more coherent text. As he does so, he explains the rationale underlying each change, but always insisting that *this is the way I would say it*, and constantly checking with the class as to what their intended meaning had been. Students then copy the reformulated text. The following page shows the text a group of Japanese students produced, and the way the teacher reformulated it.

Step 4
Students then, working individually, write their own texts about a similar topic – for example, hurricanes, volcanoes or floods. They compare these in pairs, suggesting changes and improvements, before submitting their texts to the teacher for correction.

Discussion
The teacher's intention in Step 1 is to allow the learners some say in the content and direction of the lesson and, apart from the selection of the topic, not to impose on it a prefabricated structure of his own. The joint brainstorming around a topic assumes that the class are both sufficiently forthcoming and that there is a relaxed classroom dynamic conducive to the free flow of ideas. If not, the teacher may prefer to structure this activity more purposefully, by setting a specific writing task and/or by asking leading questions. Nevertheless, as students become more accustomed to a less directive approach, they start to show more initiative.

It is important, in Step 2, that the teacher renounces any active role in the construction of the text – physically absenting himself is a clear signal that students are on their own. It is also important to establish that this is a collaborative exercise – that the class as a whole is responsible for the text,

Student text	Reformulated teacher text
Japanese and earthquake have got a quite long time relationship. More than 60 years ago the big one had occured and it caused terrible damage, for example fire which had been used for cooking at lunch time. They were quite ignorant with what they should have done. So now on that day almost all the Japanese do the situation practice against the disaster since it is predicted that the big one will surely occur before long. So that most of them keep immergent food, drink, medicine etc. Of course we hope these things are not in need.	The Japanese and earthquakes have had a long-term relationship. More than 60 years ago the 'Big One' occurred and it caused terrible damage, such as fires, due to the fact that people used fire to cook their mid-day meal. They didn't really know what precautions to take. So now, on the anniversary of that day, almost everyone in Japan does an earthquake drill, since it is predicted that the next 'Big One' will definitely occur before long. This is why most people keep emergency food, drink and medicine at home. Of course, we hope these things will not be needed.

rather than one or two of the more forthcoming individuals. If this is likely to be a problem, or if the class is too large to make this feasible, an alternative strategy would be to organise the class into groups of about four or five, and have each group produce its own text, ideally onto an overhead projector transparency, or, if not, on paper. While it will be too much for the teacher to reformulate all these texts, one or two can be chosen for the Step 3 activity.

It is important, in Step 3, that the students are involved in the text reformulation process: the teacher can elicit ideas for improvements, can ask questions to check the class's intentions, and can keep the class informed by explaining his thought processes as he hunts for better ways of expressing these intentions. Before moving into Step 4, an alternative stage might be to erase or cover up the reformulated text and ask learners to work in groups to reconstruct it from memory, using their original text as a prompt. This will force attention on form, as well as encouraging greater attentiveness during the reformulation stage.

Evaluation

The E-factor: Reformulation requires no materials preparation since the texts are created entirely by the students. All that is necessary is some stimulus, in the form, for example, of visuals, or a situation (for example, a dialogue between two friends about their health concerns), or a task (such as, Write a letter to the newspaper complaining about a local problem.) The reformulation process requires only a board, although overhead projectors are very useful for this purpose. The greatest demand is on the teacher's skill at on-the-spot reformulation. However, if the teacher has been unobtrusively present during the text construction stage, some preparation for the reformulation stage can be done in advance. In terms of **economy**, the danger is that so many problems arise out of the text there is a risk that the students lose sight of the wood because of the trees. That is, even if the teacher has pre-selected a grammatical item to focus on, and chosen a task that is likely to generate this item, it may take some time to tidy up extraneous problems before being free to home in on the target. This is not necessarily a disadvantage, however, especially at higher levels and in mixed ability classes, where a rich input rather than a purposefully lean one, is likely to be more effective in the long run: there will always be something for somebody to **notice**.

And, as with the previous example, an approach that is driven by the learners' texts is more likely to meet their immediate needs than an approach that is driven by an absentee coursebook writer.

The A-factor: For the reason just mentioned, the reformulation of learners' texts is likely to have greater relevance to learners than the study of 'imported' texts. Nevertheless, the reformulation stage has to be handled sensitively, so that learners see it as an empowering activity rather than an exercise in humiliation. Moreover, any activity that allows the teacher prolonged control of the blackboard runs the risk of becoming perilously 'chalky-talky'.

Conclusions

In this chapter we have looked at the types and causes of error, at attitudes to correction, and at strategies teachers can enlist in dealing with error. It is important to note that:

- Not all errors are caused by L1 interference. A lot of errors are developmental – that is, they occur in the normal course of language acquisition, irrespective of the learner's mother tongue.
- Not all errors are grammar errors, and not all grammar errors are simply tense mistakes.
- Not all errors matter equally: nor do they all respond to the same kind of treatment.
- Correction is not the only form of feedback that teachers can provide. Other options include positive feedback, clarification requests, and reformulation.
- Failure to provide some negative feedback may have a damaging effect on the learner's language development in the long run; on the other hand, providing only negative feedback may be ultimately demotivating.
- Learners' errors offer a rich source of material for language focus and consciousness-raising.

Looking ahead   So far we have been dealing with ways of introducing, practising, and providing feedback on grammar, and have been largely concerned with classroom activities, techniques and procedures. The view has been essentially a close-up one. But how do these activities, techniques and procedures fit into the larger context of a teacher's daily work plan? What is the place and status of grammar presentation, for example, in the overall lesson? In the next chapter we take a wider-angle view, and attempt to answer the question: How do you integrate grammar into your teaching?

8 How to integrate grammar

- The PPP model
- An alternative model
- Sample lesson 1: Integrating grammar using a PPP model of instruction
- Sample lesson 2: Integrating grammar using a task-based model of instruction
- Sample lesson 3: Integrating grammar into a skills-based lesson
- Sample lesson 4: Integrating grammar into a story-based lesson for very young learners

The PPP model

How does grammar fit into the overall context of a language lesson? Once upon a time the grammar lesson *was* the language lesson, and so the question wouldn't have been asked. Typically, lessons followed the pattern: grammar explanation followed by exercises. Or, what came to be known as **presentation** and **practice**. The practice stage was aimed at achieving accuracy. When it was recognised that accuracy alone is not enough to achieve mastery of a second language, a third element was added – **production**, the aim of which was fluency (see Chapter 6). The standard model for the language lesson became:

This kind of organisation is typical of many published English language teaching courses. It has a logic that is appealing both to teachers and learners, and it reflects the way that other skills – such as playing tennis or using a computer – are learned. That is, knowledge becomes skill through successive stages of practice. Moreover, this model allows the teacher to control the content and pace of the lesson, which, for new teachers in particular, helps them cope with the unpredictability of classroom life. It provides a convenient template onto which any number of lessons can be mapped.

Nevertheless, the PPP model has been criticised because of some of the assumptions it makes about language and language learning. It assumes, for example, that language is best learned in incremental steps, one 'bit of grammar' at a time, and that the teacher, by choosing what bit of grammar to focus on, can influence the process. Research suggests, however, that language acquisition is more complex, less linear, and less amenable to teacher intervention. The PPP model also assumes that accuracy precedes fluency. However, all learners go through a long stage of making mistakes. Meanwhile they may be perfectly capable of conveying their intended meanings fluently. As in first language learning, accuracy seems to be relatively late-acquired – a kind of fine-tuning of a system which is already up-and-running. Delaying communication until accuracy is achieved may be counterproductive. Rather than as preparation for communication, it seems that it is by means of communication that the learner's language system establishes itself and develops.

An alternative model

As we have seen, PPP represents an accuracy-to-fluency model of instruction. An alternative model stands this progression on its head, and adopts a fluency-to-accuracy sequence. Put simply, the learning cycle begins with the meanings that the learners want to convey. They try to express these meaning using their available resources. They are then given guidance as to how to do this better. This guidance may include explicit grammar instruction. Through successive stages of trial, error, and feedback, the learner's output is fine-tuned for accuracy.

Proponents of the communicative approach proposed a fluency-first model of instruction that is called **task-based**: first the learners perform a communicative task that the teacher has set them; the teacher then uses this to identify language features learners could have used in order to communicate their intentions more effectively. These features are taught and practised, before students re-perform the original (or a similar) task:

In this kind of lesson, the language items that are selected for special attention arise solely out of an assessment of the learners' communicative difficulties, rather than having been predetermined by a grammar syllabus.

But if the grammar is not pre-programmed, how is teaching organised? One approach is to organise the syllabus around the **tasks**. Thus, the syllabus objectives are expressed in terms that relate to real language **use** (telling a story, booking a hotel room etc.) rather than in grammar terms (present perfect, adverbs of frequency etc).

Task-based learning is not without its problems, however. For a start, what criteria determine the **selection** of tasks, the **ordering** of tasks, and the **evaluation** of tasks? More problematic still are the management problems associated with setting and monitoring tasks. It is partly due to these problems that task-based teaching has had a mixed reception. Nevertheless, many teachers are finding ways of marrying elements of a task-based approach with the traditional grammar syllabus.

Sample lesson

Lesson 1: Integrating grammar using a PPP model of instruction (Intermediate)

In this example, we follow a teacher as she conducts a lesson through the three stages of presentation, practice and production. The linguistic objective of the lesson is the language of coercion, e.g. the expressions *make someone do something, (not) let someone do something, be allowed to do something* and the modal structure *have to*.

Step 1

The teacher uses a generative situation (see Chapter 4, Sample lesson 3) to provide a context for the targeted language. In this case she introduces two characters, Tom and Viv, and tells the class that when he was young, Tom's parents were very strict. Viv, on the other hand, had very easygoing parents. For example, she says, *Tom had to help with the housework. But Viv didn't have to help with the housework. Tom's parents made him take piano lessons. He didn't want to, but they made him. Viv, on the other hand, wanted to have a motorbike. Her parents let her have one ...*

Step 2

The teacher asks the class to report back what they can remember her saying about Tom and Viv. She elicits on to the board the following sentences, shaping them into their correct form:

```
1  He had to help with the housework.
2  His parents made him take piano lessons.
3  He wasn't allowed to stay out late.
4  Viv didn't have to help with the housework.
5  Her parents let her have a motorbike.
6  She was allowed to stay out late.
```

Step 3

The teacher then elicits paraphrases of each of the six sentences and writes them on the board. For example:

```
1a  His parents made him help with the housework.
2a  He had to take piano lessons.
3a  They didn't let him stay out late.
```

The teacher erases the first set of sentences and asks students, in pairs, if they can reconstruct them from memory. Students write the sentences and these are read out and checked in open class.

Step 4

The teacher sets a group-work task. The object is to find out who, in their groups, went to the strictest, and who to the most easygoing, school.

Students prepare questions to ask each other using the target language forms and finally report back to the teacher. A general class discussion follows, as to the merits or not of a strict education.

Discussion

The lesson is plotted along PPP lines, with Steps 1 and 2 being the presentation, Step 3 the (controlled) practice and Step 4 the freer production. The presentation is a situational one, arguably more meaningful and memorable than a straight explanation. The teacher wastes no time in presenting learners with the written form (Step 2), since the written form is more easily processed than the spoken form and therefore a better medium for a grammar focus.

The practice stages involve the students first of all transforming and then reconstructing the **model** sentences (Step 3). Again, this is done as a written exercise, allowing students reflection time as well as the chance to work collaboratively. It is probably at the stage when the students are reading out their sentences that the teacher would start to fine-tune for accurate pronunciation. The fluency task (Step 4) is still relatively controlled, but by having the students ask and answer a lot of questions using the target language there is built-in repetition. Moreover, there is a communicative purpose to the task, ensuring a focus on meaning as much as on form.

Evaluation

The E-factor: A PPP model is an **easy** one to use and adapt, as was pointed out earlier. In terms of **economy**, i.e. the learning dividends measured against the time and effort involved, the PPP model scores less highly. This is in part because it is too easy to over-prolong the first P at the expense of the other two. There is always something more that can be said about a point of grammar: a case of grammar expanding to fill the time available for it. As a rough rule-of-thumb the proportion of time spent on each of the three stages of PPP in a lesson should be something like 1:2:3.

It is the **efficacy** of PPP that is most disputed. Many of the problems have been outlined earlier in this chapter, and rather than review them, it may be more instructive to compare Sample lesson 1 with Sample lesson 2 which follows.

The A-factor: The PPP model reflects most students' experience of classroom instruction whatever the subject: the progression from theory to practice has an unassailable logic. This, of course, does not mean that it is the most effective model, but teachers should not be surprised if they encounter resistance when applying alternative models. What is inappropriate, however, is to turn the PPP model into an excuse for copious teacher explanation – the infamous 'chalk-and-talk' school of teaching (see Chapter 10).

Sample lesson

Lesson 2: Integrating grammar using a task-based model of instruction (Intermediate)

How could the lesson in Sample lesson 1 be recast to fit a task-based model? In the following lesson, at the same level, the same notional area (coercion) and the same theme (childhood) are dealt with in a wholly different way, one which is driven by the learners' meanings, rather than the teacher's grammar agenda.

Step 1

The teacher introduces the theme by telling a short anecdote about her school days, which demonstrates, for example, the relaxed approach to the dress-code operating in her school. She uses this story to check the meaning of *easygoing* and its opposite, *strict*.

Step 2

The teacher invites one or two learners to recount related experiences. She suggests that many people react against a strict upbringing by adopting very easygoing attitudes as parents, and vice versa. Since there is some argument about this, she suggests that the class conduct a survey, in which they canvass each other to see if there is any correlation between previous experience and present attitudes. She organises the class into pairs to prepare questions, which they write down.

Step 3

The teacher organises the pairs of students into groups of four, and asks them to try out their questions on each other, and to make a mental note of the answers. She monitors the interactions, noting down examples of student productions that could be improved, but she doesn't correct them at this point.

Step 4

The teacher asks the class to listen to a recording of some fluent English speakers chatting on the same theme. The conversation includes various examples of the language of coercion. The teacher asks some general gist questions about the conversation – for example, which of the speakers had a strict upbringing, which had an easygoing one? She then hands out a transcript of the recording, and replays the tape while they read.

Step 5

Students then study the transcript with a view to finding language that might be useful in the survey task, particularly language related to the notions of being strict and easygoing. They list these in two columns: adjectives and verbs. Students work in pairs on this task, and then the teacher elicits ideas on to the board. For example:

```
ADJECTIVES          VERBS
tolerant            I was allowed  .....................
                    he made me     .....................
                    I won't let them  .....................
```

She then asks the class to complete the blank spaces after each verb, and to make generalisations about the grammar of the verbs. She also elicits the question forms of the verb structures: *were you allowed to ...?* etc.

Step 6

The students then return to their survey task – but are first given a chance to redraft and refine their questions in pairs. They are then paired off with different students than the ones they were talking to earlier (in Step 3).

Step 7

The teacher then asks students, working in their original pairs, to prepare a report on their findings, with a view to answering the question: How does upbringing affect attitudes? Individual students are asked to present their report to the class. A general discussion ensues.

Discussion

The lesson is a task-based one because, rather than being plotted around a pre-selected item of grammar, the purpose of the lesson is to achieve a task outcome: in this case, deciding how upbringing affects attitudes. While this may seem contrived – just as contrived, in fact, as pre-selecting a grammar item – it could be argued that the task focus encourages learners to take more creative risks with their language. They needn't restrict themselves to the teacher's grammar agenda (as in Sample lesson 1): theoretically, they could choose any language from the sample text (Step 4). Finally, and most importantly, a task invests the lesson with an intrinsic interest, apart from a concern only for language. The language is simply a means, not an end in itself (as is so often the case in PPP-type lessons).

It should be clear that this task-based lesson shares many of the ingredients of the PPP lesson, but that the order is radically different: the major difference being that the production stage is brought to the front of the lesson (Steps 2 and 3) after an initial introduction to the theme (Step 1). The lesson starts in the deep end, as it were. The production stage acts as a trial run, where learners attempt to put into words the meanings they wish to express. The problems they have doing this should motivate them to look for solutions in the sample text (Step 4). That is, they have an incentive to use the text as a resource, and may be better primed for **noticing** features of the text than if they had just read it for the sake of reading it. The teacher's role is to guide students (Step 5) to notice features that she herself has diagnosed as being misused or underused in the trial run. Students are then ready, theoretically, to re-attempt the task (Step 6). As a final push towards accuracy, the **report stage** (Step 7), in which the students 'go public', imposes an element of formality that forces attention on to form.

Evaluation

The E-factor: A task-based lesson generally requires more in the way of classroom management than a lesson in which learners are led through a succession of practice activities. This is because it invariably involves some degree of peer interaction and collaboration. In addition, there is an element of unpredictability in lessons that begin with a diagnostic activity, out of which the language focus emerges. Of course, experienced teachers are generally good improvisers. More usefully still, they are capable of predicting (and therefore preparing for) the kind of language problems their learners are likely to encounter in engaging in a task. Nevertheless, the management demands, and the likelihood of having to 'think on their feet', make a task-based approach a risky undertaking for new teachers, or for teachers of large classes. Moreover, the lack of task-based materials means that teachers who wish to adopt this approach will have to adapt existing materials or create their own. And designing a task that will be motivating, manageable, and language productive, requires some ingenuity. A task-based approach, then, is not **easy**.

Nor is it necessarily any more **economical** in terms of time and resources than a PPP lesson. The two lessons that have been described – Sample lessons 1 and 2 – probably would take about the same length of time to execute.

When it comes to **efficacy**, however, there is reason to rate a task-based approach highly. For a start, a task-based lesson usually engages the learner more than a grammar-based one. This means there is likely to be a greater depth of language processing, not to mention greater interest and motivation. Also, the principle underlying the trial run is that learners are more likely to notice language features in the input that they themselves have discovered a need for, rather than language features that have simply been served up to them. And, while some learners will notice feature A in the input stage, others will notice feature B, and still others feature C, whereas in a PPP approach the much narrower focus reduces the chances of incidental learning considerably. Finally, a task-based approach, by offering the learners an opportunity to make meanings for themselves, seems to replicate more closely natural acquisition approaches, in which accuracy develops out of fluency and not the other way round. The danger of such a meaning-driven approach is that features of form may go unnoticed and that the learner's output becomes fluent but inaccurate. In the worst-case scenario **fossilisation** may set in. To guard against this, frequent overtly form-focused stages need to be built in to the task-cycle.

The A-factor: As was suggested above, learners are more likely to be used to the well-trodden PPP path than to task-based learning. Nevertheless, a task-based approach would seem to be particularly appropriate with learners at an intermediate level and above, who have a grounding in basic grammar and vocabulary, but need opportunities to put this language to use. It also works well with mixed ability groups, since task achievement does not depend on having a specific level of ability: it is rather a case of 'each according to their means'.

To sum up, then, a presentation (PPP) approach is based on the premise that there is something that the learners don't know and it attempts to fill these holes in their knowledge. A task-based approach, on the other hand, starts from the assumption that there is something that the learners can do and it attempts to empower them with the means to do this more effectively.

Sample lesson

Lesson 3: Integrating grammar into a skills-based lesson (Intermediate)

Although in the preceding two examples we have gone to some lengths to contrast presentation-based and task-based models of instruction, it may be misleading to give the impression that it is a case of one or the other. The following example attempts to demonstrate that, although the teacher is working to a grammar syllabus, it is possible to incorporate the targeted language into a lesson that is essentially a skills one – that is, a lesson whose primary focus is the development of listening, reading, speaking or writing skills.

Step 1

The teacher tells the class an adventure he had in a North African country, when he was travelling with a group of friends. While he is telling the story (and, note, telling, not reading) he is also recording it on a personal stereo. Into the story he inserts, unobtrusively, a number of examples of the structure *so* + adjective *that ...* as in *It was so hot that we decided to go for a swim ... the people were so friendly that we didn't want to leave ... the train was so crowded that we couldn't find a seat ...* Once the story is completed, the students respond, asking questions to clarify details of the story and adding comments of their own.

Step 2

The teacher then asks questions on details of the story. For example, he asks *What did I say about the weather?* The students respond as well as they can remember, for example *It was very hot; It was too hot.* The teacher rewinds the tape of the recording to the appropriate point, and asks them to listen: *It was so hot that we decided to go for a swim ...* He continues by asking similar questions such as *What did I say about the people? About the train?* and each time finding the point in the recording where he uses the *so ... that* construction. Each instance of the structure is written on the board.

Step 3

The teacher then produces a copy of a letter, telling the class that this is the letter he wrote to his parents, recounting the incident. He asks them to guess which parts of the story he didn't tell his parents or that he may have altered. He hands out copies of the letter so that they can see if their predictions were right. They read and then report on the differences between the 'true' narrative and the version he gave his parents.

Step 4

The teacher then asks the students to tell him what he had written about the weather. The students try *It was so hot that you decided to go for a swim.* He asks them to check the letter, where in fact he has written *It was such a hot day we decided to go for a swim.* He repeats the sequence of questions with regard to the people, the train etc, and each time the students find that, where the spoken narrative had *so* + adjective + *that* ... the written text has *such (a)* + adjective + noun + *that* ... Each instance of this latter construction is written on the board alongside its equivalent construction from the spoken text. For example:

> It was so hot that we decided to go for a swim.   It was such a hot day that we ...

Step 5

The teacher asks students to formulate the rule. He writes it up in this form:

> so + adjective + that ...
> such (a) + adjective + noun + that ...

Step 6

The teacher then clears the board of the sentences, leaving only the above rules, and asks the students to write a short summary of his story, incorporating the sentences they have been studying. They do this individually, and then compare their stories in pairs.

Step 7

The teacher invites students to recall similar incidents that may have happened to them or to someone they know. They tell their stories, first to each other in pairs, and then selected students are asked to tell their story to the class. Where the teacher sees an opportunity to incorporate the use of *so* or *such* he pauses the story and elicits the appropriate construction from other students.

Discussion

In essence this is a PPP lesson, with the targeted language presented by means of a text – or, in fact, two texts (Steps 1 and 3) – followed by a short practice stage (Step 6) and a production stage (Step 7). Nevertheless, the lesson is so rich in skills work that it hardly seems like a grammar lesson at all. It is much more like a task-based lesson, the task being to tell and compare travel stories. And yet the grammar is fed in and recycled consistently throughout, and is made sufficiently 'problematic' (Step 4) that the students cannot fail to notice it. By using his own story, the teacher virtually guarantees a high level of engagement on the part of the students;

this is enhanced by his telling it rather than simply reading it aloud: in this way he is able both to monitor student understanding more directly and to make on-line adjustments where understanding seems to have faltered. Moreover, by recording it, he has the text available for later language-focused work (Step 2). Because this lesson involved a contrast between two similar structures, the teacher has used two texts, but this is an added extra to a lesson format that can be reduced to this basic formula:

In this model, the first text is the teacher's text, and the second is the student's. The language that is taught is taken from the first text and reintegrated into the second. In the case of the sample lesson, any number of features of narrative could have been chosen to focus on – for example, the use of sequencing devices such as *then, eventually, meanwhile* etc. As it happened, the teacher, working from a grammar-based syllabus that prescribes what he is to teach, used the narrative as a vehicle for introducing *so* and *such*.

Evaluation

The E-factor and the A-factor: It requires little ingenuity to structure a lesson around your own story, whether it is a holiday narrative, your daily routine, a future plan, a childhood memory, or the layout of your flat. In fact it is highly unlikely that there is any language area that cannot be turned into **teacher text**. For teachers who have no access to authentic materials, using their own texts would seem to be not only the most realistic solution, but the most effective. The teacher's text also provides a model for the students' texts, both at the level of the type of text and at the level of the specific language features embedded in it. Again, in terms of priming the students as to what they will have to do, a **text–teach–text** model is **easy** and **economical**.

Recording the text while telling it adds a technical complication, but the pay-off is considerable in terms of the potential for language-focused work. An alternative might be to write a script of the text in advance of the lesson, read it aloud and then provide learners with copies of the transcript. But this would be at the expense of naturalness and spontaneity. A compromise is to pre-script the text, and rehearse it sufficiently so that it can be told (not read) as naturally as possible.

In terms of overall **efficacy** as well as **appropriacy**, the approach combines advantages of a PPP approach (in that it is compatible with a grammar syllabus) and of a task-based approach, in that there is a heavy emphasis on skills, on fluency (both receptive and productive), and on meaning. Of course, the efficacy is going to depend to a large extent on the teacher's ability to provide sufficient highlighting of the targeted language items without letting this stage become the lesson.

Sample lesson

Lesson 4: Integrating grammar into a story-based lesson for very young learners

Most of the approaches so far have been targeted at adult or young adult learners. This is largely because any explicit focus on grammar is going to be over the heads of learners younger than eleven or twelve years old. The research evidence suggests that until learners reach this age, second language acquisition *is* acquisition, and that the new language is best experienced rather than learned. Stories and songs offer a language-rich and highly engaging means of experiencing the language.

In this lesson, the teacher of a group of five-year-olds is incorporating the present perfect continuous into a story-telling activity.

Step 1

The teacher is seated and the children sit in a half-circle on a mat at her feet. She uses a series of large visual aids to tell the story of Goldilocks and the Three Bears. The visuals can take the form of either a 'big book' or a set of loose-leaf pictures, but they are big enough to be seen clearly by all the children. The story is told naturally but clearly, and with a good deal of checking of understanding (*OK?*) and of repetition. She also stops to explain or translate unfamiliar vocabulary as it occurs. The teacher inserts frequent examples of the present perfect continuous into the story, in the form of statements (*Someone's been eating my porridge*) and of questions (*Who's been eating my porridge?*), and adapts the traditional story so as to be able to include several instances of this: *Who's been drinking my milk? Who's been reading my newspaper? Who's been sitting in my chair? Who's been playing with my doll?* etc. A typical sequence might go like this:

> 'And then Father Bear found his newspaper. His newspaper was all mixed up [teacher gestures appropriately]. Father Bear thought *Someone's been reading my newspaper*. Father Bear asked *Who's been reading my newspaper? ...*'

Step 2

The teacher goes through the story again, this time inviting the children to chorus the refrain *Who's been eating my porridge?* etc.

Step 3

The teacher repeats the story in subsequent lessons, and, at each successive telling, she invites more and more participation from the children. She also varies the story by either re-arranging the sequence, or by introducing new elements, such as further evidence of Goldilocks having been in the house (*Someone's been using my computer; someone's been picking my flowers ... etc*). The children are eventually so familiar with the story that, prompted mainly by the pictures, they are capable of telling it on their own.

Step 4

The teacher sets the children the task of drawing their own pictures for the story, which they can use as a basis for re-telling.

Discussion

The sequence adopts the same approach to text-familiarisation that children experience in their first language: that is, repeated tellings, reinforced with visual stimuli and such theatrical elements as changes of voice (*Who's been eating my porridge?*). Into these re-tellings a number of repeated, refrain-like elements are incorporated. No attempt is made to deal with the text or the language embedded in it as an object in its own right, e.g. by talking about the grammar. The principle operating is that, at this age, engaging and comprehensible input is sufficient to trigger acquisition.

For very young learners, there seems no limit to the amount of repeated tellings of a story they will tolerate, although these tellings should be spread over a number of lessons. As they get older, however, this tolerance drops off markedly. The teacher will then need to find tasks that disguise the repetitive element, by, for example, having them transform the story in some way, such as turning it into the script of a puppet play, or telling it backwards, or telling it from the point of view of another character.

Evaluation

The E-factor: For the stories to be meaningful and engaging they will need to be reinforced with some visual element: pictures, puppets, stick figures on the board, building blocks, mime, video, etc. This may require considerable preparation on the part of the teacher. However, once prepared the material can be used and re-used, and, as noted above, there is no limit to young children's tolerance for repetition. More challenging is to find stories that have refrain-like elements, or, in the absence of these, to adapt traditional stories to include a high turnover of such formulaic language.

Stories provide a textual **scaffold** that supports the introduction of language that may be way beyond the learner's capacity to process and produce. Children have an enviable capacity to cope with 'fuzzy' meaning – that is, they are much less bothered than adults might be by vocabulary that they don't understand, so long as the overall shape of the story is familiar. The efficacy of stories as a means of introducing young learners to a new language is beyond doubt, and there is no shortage of stories. The challenge, perhaps, is to persuade their parents that stories and songs are a more efficient route to language acquisition than the study of grammar.

The A-factor: Story-telling is **appropriate** to all ages and all cultures, and works just as well with large classes as with small ones, provided that all students can see the visual stimuli, and that the teacher involves all the students. As pointed out above, the extent to which children will tolerate repeated hearings of the same story will depend on their age. Moreover, stories may need to be chosen carefully to avoid cultural unfamiliarity, or, more controversially, elements that might distress children, or that might promote the formation of negative stereotypes.

Conclusion In this chapter we have taken a wider-angle view of the role of grammar, and looked at it from the perspective of the design of lessons as a whole, attempting to answer the question: How does grammar fit into a lesson? Two contrastive models of lesson design have been examined: the PPP model, and the task-based one. Each of these derives from a different theory of learning, the major claims of each theory being:

In the PPP model
• language is learned in bits and in steps
• fluency develops out of accuracy
• grammatical knowledge is proceduralised through practice

In the task-based model
• language is acquired in lumps and in leaps
• accuracy develops after fluency
• the internal grammar develops through exposure and interaction

We have also seen how certain pedagogical characteristics of each model can be combined in lessons which are skills- or text-based, and in which, while the primary focus is on meaning, sufficient attention is given to form to satisfy the demands of a grammar syllabus. This form-focus can be explicit, or implicit, as in the case of story-telling for very young learners.

Looking ahead We have now looked at ways of presenting grammar, of practising it, and of integrating it into the curriculum. One important question remains unaddressed: How do you test it? In the next chapter we examine the issues and look at some practical examples.

How to test grammar

- **Grammar testing**
- **Sample test 1: Testing grammar using discrete-item tests**
- **Sample test 2: Testing grammar in an oral performance test**

Grammar testing

You have taught the grammar. You have practised it. You have corrected it. But how do you know if the process has worked? How do you test it?

Grammar is typically tested by means of what are called **discrete-item tests**. That is, the individual components of the learner's knowledge (for example, irregular past tense verb forms such as *went*, *saw*, *did* etc.) are tested using tasks such as gap-fills:

> Yesterday we [1] _____ to the cinema and [2] _____ a film with Richard Gere in it.

Or multiple choice tasks:

> Yesterday we [1] (go/went/have gone) _____ to the cinema and
>
> [2] (see/saw/have seen) _____ a film with Richard Gere in it.

Tests of this sort make up a significant proportion of what passes as grammar testing – and, indeed, language testing generally – whether the purpose of the test is to place learners in the right class (**placement tests**), to test how they are getting on mid-course (**progress tests**), or to test how well they have done at the end (**achievement tests**). One of the attractions of these kinds of test is that they are relatively easy to design and they are very easy to set and mark: they are **practical**. And, importantly, they meet learners' expectations as to what a test should be like: they have what is called **face validity**. (If a test lacks face validity, i.e. if it isn't recognisable as a test, students may under-perform or contest the results.) They also fulfil another criterion of test effectiveness in that they are **reliable**. That is, the results are consistent, regardless of who marks them, and the same students tend to get the same results on similar tests. They are also **valid** tests if all we want to test is the learner's knowledge of a specific area. For example, a diagnostic test of specific grammar items may be helpful in planning the grammar component of a course for a particular group of learners. And

141

having taught an item of grammar it would make sense to test it before moving on to something new. For progress testing of grammar learning, therefore, discrete-item tests of grammar have a useful role to play. Apart from anything else, they will motivate learners to go back and review what they have been studying. Finally, they have positive **spin-off**. That is to say, they can be used in class subsequently for reviewing specific areas of difficulty. This means that testing can be a learning experience as well.

As tests of overall language proficiency, however, such tests leave a lot to be desired. They do not really provide the kind of information necessary to make a rounded assessment of the learner's abilities. For example, they do not give any information as to the learner's ability to **communicate**, including how well the learner can cope in situations of real-life language use. While it is useful to know what the learner knows, to test only for knowledge (i.e. **competence**) without also testing the **ability to use** that knowledge is like setting a driving test that consists only of a written test of the Highway Code.

The language-testing equivalent of a valid driving test would need to show how well the learner can 'drive' in the language: it would need to be a **performance test**. What does this mean in practice? Does it mean that, if we want to test if a learner can order a meal, we send him to the nearest restaurant? Theoretically, yes, but in practice this would be far too impractical. As an alternative we might set up a situation in class – a role play – which involved ordering a meal. This is fine for testing a functional objective, like ordering a meal, but here we are concerned with grammar testing. How do you test, say, past simple questions in performance? One solution, perhaps, is to think of a situation which could be role-played in the classroom and which would require the use of past simple questions. As an example, two students could interview each other with a view to finding out how similar or how different their last weekend was. It would be difficult to do this task without needing to use past tense questions.

This sounds practical – just – but it is a far remove from the convenience of gap-fills and multiple choice. Performance testing is not as practical as competence testing. Nor is it as easy for examiners to agree on how to rate performance, hence it is less reliable. One particular advantage of performance testing, however, is that it reminds teachers that language teaching is more than simply teaching the grammar – it is also teaching the ability to use the grammar. From this point of view, performance testing has a useful **backwash effect** – that is to say, in preparing for this kind of test, as much classroom time will be spent on communication as on grammar.

So, while there are very good reasons for incorporating performance tests into a teaching programme, there are also good – if more pragmatic – reasons for sticking to discrete-item competence tests. Ideally, both kinds of test could be used, either in conjunction, or at different stages of the learning cycle. For example, a discrete-item test could be given immediately after the first introduction of a new grammar item. Later, to test how well the learners have integrated the item and how readily and accurately they can use it, a performance test would be appropriate.

To sum up, then: there are six factors that need to be taken into account when assessing the value of a test:

- Its practicality – how easy is it to set up, administer, and mark?
- Its reliability – does it give consistent results, e.g. do the results tally with those of similar students, and when marked by different people?
- Its validity – does it test what we want to test, and not something else?
- Its face validity – do the students recognise it as a fair test, and will they therefore perform to their ability?
- Backwash – does it positively influence the teaching that will be done in preparation for it?
- Spin-off – can the test be used subsequently for review and remedial teaching?

Where discrete-item tests lose points with regard to their overall validity, they are more reliable, practical and, from the student's point of view, they look like tests. They can also be used afterwards for review purposes. Their backwash effect is less powerful than that of performance tests, however.

Sample test

Test 1: Testing grammar using discrete-item tests

The teacher of an intermediate class has been working on the differences between *yet*, *already* and *still* – adverbs that present problems not only in terms of meaning but also in terms of syntax, that is, their position in the sentence and the kinds of verb structures they combine with. The teacher now wishes to test her students' command of these adverbs. She can't decide between the following five short tests:

1

In each sentence choose the best place (/) to put the word in brackets:

1	The 7.25 train / hasn't / arrived /.	(still)
2	/ Haven't you / done your homework / ?	(yet)
3	I / have / sent / all my Christmas cards.	(already)
4	/ Ben / is / doing his homework.	(still)
5	How many cookies / have / you eaten / ?	(already)
6	/ The film / hasn't started /.	(yet)

2

Complete this text with *yet*, *still*, or *already*:

Preparations are underway for the Pan-World Games in Lomoka next year. Many new hotels have [1] _____ been built and tourists are [2] _____ making reservations. But the main stadium hasn't been started [3] _____ . They are [4] _____ deciding where to put it. The Athletes' Village is [5] _____ being built, and the swimming complex isn't completed [6] _____ .

3

Look at the information in the chart and decide if the sentences are true or false.

WORLD CUP UPDATE

Morocco–Tunisia ____	USA–Germany: in progress
S. Korea–Morocco ____	Japan–Austria: in progress
Croatia–England 0–0	Austria–USA 3–0
Tunisia–Croatia 3–1	Germany–Japan 0–0
Morocco–England 2–1	Austria–Germany 1–1

1 England have already played Morocco.
2 Tunisia haven't played Croatia yet.
3 Japan still haven't played a match.
4 The United States have already lost once.
5 South Korea haven't played yet.
6 Germany still haven't scored a goal.

4

Complete these sentences to make true statements:

1 Scientists still haven't_____.
2 People have already_____.
3 Explorers have already _____.
4 My teacher has already _____.
5 My best friend_____ yet.
6 I am still _____.

5

Write a letter to a friend of between 75 and 100 words. Ask him/her about their news, and tell them some news of your own. Include two examples each of *yet, still* and *already*.

Discussion and evaluation

Before discussing these individual tests, it may be helpful to re-define the E-factor (efficiency) and the A-factor (appropriacy) in the terminology associated with testing. The **ease** and **economy** factors are issues of **practicality**. The **efficacy** of a test relates to its **reliability, validity, backwash effect** and **spin-off**. The **face validity** of a test needs to be assessed in terms of the learners' assessment of its **appropriacy**.

Test 1 is fairly limited in that it tests only the students' knowledge of the word order constraints on the three adverbs. It is conceivable that students could do the test without understanding either the meaning of the adverbs themselves nor the contexts into which they have to put them. To improve the validity of this test (i.e. so that it tests what the tester is interested in testing), it would need to be supported by an exercise that tests learners' ability to distinguish the meaning, not only the form, of the adverbs. Asking students to translate the sentences into their mother tongue (in the case of a monolingual group) might be one choice; alternatively, any of the more meaning-focused exercises that follow would do as well. A further problem with this test is that, because it is essentially a multiple choice exercise (there are three choices of correct adverb placement), the student has a reasonable chance of getting at least a third of the answers right purely through random guesswork. One way around this problem would be not to indicate the possible adverb positions:

1 The 7.25 train hasn't arrived.   (still)
2 Haven't you done your homework?   (yet)
3 I have sent all my Christmas cards.   (already)

Test 2 is the classic gap-fill type of exercise and has the added advantage of being a whole text rather than isolated sentences. The learner – in order to fill the gaps successfully – has to attend to the meaning of the text, although, since the testee has only three choices of adverb in each case, chance can play a part in getting the answer right. Nevertheless, this kind of test is relatively easy to design, and extremely easy to mark, hence its wide popularity in progress tests of this type.

It should not be confused with what is called a **cloze test**. A true cloze test is a text in which every *n*th word has been deleted – e.g. every seventh, or every ninth, or whatever – so that the item deleted is not pre-selected. A cloze test tests much more than knowledge of one discrete-item, as this example (where, after an initial run-up, every seventh word is deleted) demonstrates:

> Preparations are underway for the Pan-World Games in Lomoka next year. Many new hotels have [1] _____ been built and tourists are already [2] _____ reservations. But the main stadium hasn't [3] _____ started yet. They are still deciding [4] _____ to put it. The Athletes' Village [5] _____ still being built, and the swimming [6] _____ isn't completed yet ...

Cloze tests are effective at testing overall linguistic competence, but because they capture a wide variety of language items and therefore test a wide range of competences (grammar, vocabulary, and discourse) they seem to work better as placement tests, where an overall assessment of a learner's competence is needed, than as progress tests, where specific syllabus items are being targeted. For this reason, a 'selective cloze' (as in example Test 2) is preferred for progress testing, where pre-selected items (such as all the prepositions, or all the past tense verbs) are gapped out.

The main problem with both Tests 1 and 2 is that they are primarily form-focused rather than meaning-focused. That is, the student could do both tests simply by knowing where *still*, *yet* and *already* go in the sentence, but without having much understanding of what they mean. One way of getting around this is the approach adopted in Test 3, where students have to match their understanding of the meaning of the test item against some data. Test 3 tests the learners' understanding of the items and is a kind of **grammar interpretation** task (see Chapter 6). The assumption underlying a comprehension test is that the tester is not at this early stage expecting students to be able to produce the targeted items accurately since there is inevitably a time lag between understanding and production. It would, of course, be quite easy to turn this test into a grammar production test, by changing the instructions to the following:

> Look at the information in the chart and make ten sentences with *yet*, *already* and *still*. Include at least two examples of each.

Tests 4 and 5 allow a considerable degree of freedom to the student, which makes for marking problems. But by providing less contrived contexts for displaying the targeted items, and by requiring production as well as comprehension, these tests move in the direction of performance tests. Test 4 requires the learner to exercise a little imagination, and therefore would not favour students who find spontaneity and creativity – especially under test conditions – a tall order. Of the two tests, the second (Test 5) provides a more natural context, but, again, will favour students who are already good writers, and who have a flexible vocabulary at their command. This reduces the effectiveness of the test as a discrete-item one. The marker may need to take this into account, awarding marks for correct instances of the targeted items, but not deducting marks for other errors.

The above test types by no means exhaust the range of tests that can be used for testing progress on grammar learning. Different grammar items will lend themselves to different kinds of tests, and a selection of test types will work better than one alone. Whatever test-type is chosen, it is important that students are familiar with it in advance. In fact, all the above tests make perfectly valid exercise types for pair and group work as well as for individual study, and in this sense they can have positive **backwash effects**. A good way of familiarising students with different test types is to get them, in groups, to design their own, which they then use to test each other. A quick review of some standard test types is all that is needed to get them going. This not only helps demystify the tests, but provides a useful focus for revision.

Sample test

Test 2: Testing grammar in an oral performance test

The kind of tests we have looked at so far have taken the close-up view, testing bits of grammar in isolation, without testing whether the student has integrated these isolated bits of knowledge into a functioning system. What do they really tell us about what the learner can do? To return to the driving analogy, this is like testing a driver solely on the basis of their knowledge of the road rules. Or, in terms of the familiar PPP model, it is like doing only controlled practice activities without doing production ones.

This suggests that, if discrete-item tests are modelled on practice activities, then performance tests could be modelled on the standard repertoire of classroom production activities. In other words, role plays, simulations, discussions – even informal chat – may provide useful test tasks. The main problem is in deciding the criteria of assessment and then in applying them.

In this example, the teacher has been working with a lower intermediate class on the language of description of places, including describing changes using the present perfect (*They've built a new bridge*). He decides to test this using an oral interaction activity.

Step 1
The students are divided into pairs, and, while the rest of the class is working on a writing activity, each pair takes turns to leave the classroom and go to an adjoining room for the test. Each member of the pair is given a copy of either the STUDENT A or the STUDENT B picture (see page 148). Neither student is allowed to see their partner's picture. They are allowed time to read the instructions and to study their pictures.

Step 2
With the examiner present (perhaps another teacher), the students perform the activity, taking turns to describe their own picture, and then to work out what has changed. The examiner listens and scores each student according to the following criteria:

Fluency (including fluidity of speech and ability to interact)

hesitant				fluid
1	2	3	4	5

interacts poorly				interacts well
1	2	3	4	5

Complexity (including syntactic complexity and vocabulary range)

simple syntax				complex syntax
1	2	3	4	5

limited vocabulary				extensive vocabulary
1	2	3	4	5

Accuracy (including pronunciation and grammar)

highly accented				slightly accented
1	2	3	4	5

inaccurate grammar				accurate grammar
1	2	3	4	5

Total: _____ out of 30.

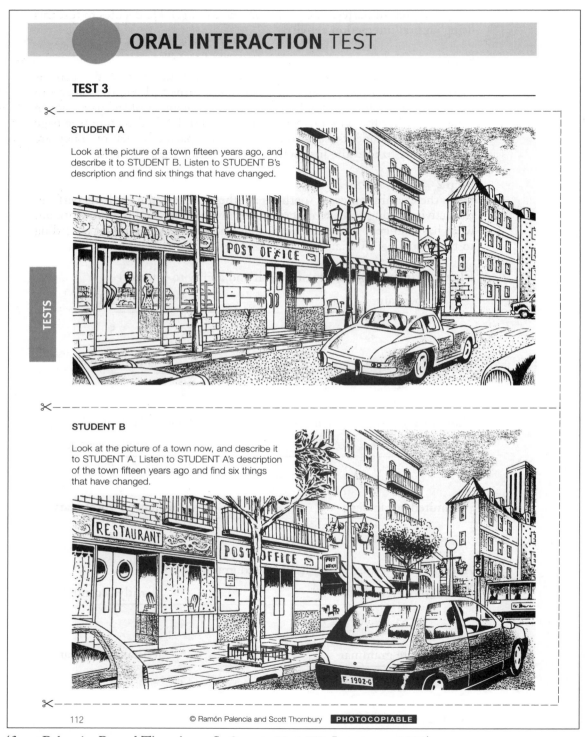

ORAL INTERACTION TEST

TEST 3

STUDENT A

Look at the picture of a town fifteen years ago, and describe it to STUDENT B. Listen to STUDENT B's description and find six things that have changed.

BREAD

POST OFFICE

SHOP

STUDENT B

Look at the picture of a town now, and describe it to STUDENT A. Listen to STUDENT A's description of the town fifteen years ago and find six things that have changed.

RESTAURANT

POST OFFICE

SHOP

F-1902-G

112 © Ramón Palencia and Scott Thornbury **PHOTOCOPIABLE**

TESTS

(from Palencia, R. and Thornbury, S. *Over to Us 4, TB*, Longman, 1998)

148

Discussion and evaluation

The teacher has chosen an information gap task in order to simulate the conditions of authentic language use (see Chapter 6). The need to 'cross the gap' obliges the students to put their communicative resources to the test. One component of these resources is their ability to use the linguistic system (grammar, vocabulary and pronunciation) for communicative purposes. This type of test, then, has positive **backwash effects**, in that, in order to prepare for it, the students will need practice in interaction skills as well as in the grammar itself. It is also a **valid** test, in that, assuming the teacher's overall teaching aim is to develop his students' communicative competence, the test is consistent with the course objectives.

More problematic is the validity of the scoring system itself and particularly the weighting given to the different categories. Does, for example, the equal distribution of marks between fluency, complexity and accuracy truly reflect the balance of knowledge and skills required to do the task successfully? And is the distinction between accuracy and complexity a valid one? (In Chapter 6 we argued that it was.)

Other problems raised by the scoring system relate to the issue of **reliability**. Are the categories sufficiently differentiated or do they overlap? Are more detailed descriptions needed for each criterion? To what extent does a subjective, impressionistic element enter into the evaluation? Would two different scorers give the same or similar marks?

One way of improving the reliability of the test is to have different testers score a sample of the tests. Where there is a marked difference in scores between testers, the criteria for assessment may need to be renegotiated.

The **face validity** of the test may also be questionable, especially if students think that their performance is dependent on their partner's. An alternative might be to do the task with the examiner, or, if available, another teacher, while the examiner listens. Finally, in terms of **spin-off**, there is not a lot the teacher can do with this kind of test afterwards in class, unless it has been recorded somehow.

Even if all these problems are ironed out, there is still the question of **practicality**. As was pointed out earlier, this kind of test is much more difficult to set up, administer and score than the discrete-item tests customarily used to test grammar knowledge.

Nevertheless, the fact that this kind of test is much more consistent with the objectives of a communicative teaching programme suggests that it is worth trying, at least from time to time, and especially when assessing a learner's overall achievement at the end of a course. A sensible compromise might be to use oral performance tests in conjunction with discrete-item tests, rather than as an alternative.

Conclusion   Testing is a headache – so much so that some teachers and institutions avoid it altogether. However, since tests are a recognised means of providing both teacher and learner with feedback on the teaching/learning process, and since they are a useful means of encouraging learners to review, they can have a positive influence on language learning. Many students may be interested in preparing for public examinations, so regular testing, both formal and informal, helps familiarise them with the different methods and conditions of assessment. It is important, however, that testing be done well – or as well as possible. Insofar as this affects the testing of grammar the teacher needs to ask the following questions:

- Does this test assess what the learners know or what they can do with that knowledge? Both kinds of test are valid, but a test of knowledge cannot fairly be used to test use.
- Has the learner been sufficiently prepared for the test and does it reflect the learner's classroom experience?
- Will the test be as much a learning experience as a testing one?

Looking ahead   So far we have attempted to ask the question: How do you teach grammar? This has involved considering how learners learn grammar, how practice influences learning, and how learning is tested. On the way, we have looked at a range of presentation approaches, a range of practice and testing activities, and a range of ways of integrating grammar into the language lesson. Such a range, in fact, that the impression may have been given that 'anything goes'. It might be useful, therefore to consider whether there are any ways in which grammar should not be taught. That is the purpose of the final chapter.

How NOT to teach grammar

- **Sample lesson: How not to teach the past perfect**
- **Some rules**
- **Some conditions**
- **Some caveats**

This chapter will be short because a) there are very many more options for teaching grammar well than there are for teaching it badly, and b) it should be clear by now what this book considers to be ineffective grammar teaching, so a lengthy rehearsal of the arguments is probably unnecessary. This chapter, then, will stand as a short summary of what has gone before, and will attempt to answer the question implied in the title, that is: How do you teach grammar?

First of all, let's look at a lesson. The teacher is teaching a group of intermediate level teenagers:

Sample lesson

Lesson: How not to teach the past perfect (Intermediate)

Step 1

The teacher introduces the lesson by telling the class that they are going to have a grammar lesson. He writes on the board 'past perfect'. He then explains the rules of formation and use of the past perfect (as in *he had worked* ...), including how the past perfect is used to refer to a time anterior to an established past reference, and how the past perfect is also used in reported speech to transform direct speech instances of the past simple and the present perfect. He also points out that the past perfect functions in conditional clauses to refer to hypothetical past time (as in *If I had known you were coming* ...).

Step 2

He asks if the class understands, and then distributes an exercise, which involves converting past simple and present perfect structures into the past perfect, as:

I went to the beach → I had gone to the beach.
She has seen the movie → She had seen the movie.

The students work on this individually and then take turns to read their answers out aloud. The teacher corrects any errors.

Step 3

In the remaining ten minutes of the lesson, the teacher sets up a game of 'Hangman', the vocabulary game in which the class are allowed several guesses at the gapped-out letters of a word.

Discussion and evaluation

First of all, let's be generous to the teacher and allow him the benefit of the doubt – it probably wasn't his decision to include the past perfect as an isolated item in the syllabus. Nevertheless, the past perfect is rarely if ever found in isolation, but instead co-exists with other tenses, and functions so as to avoid ambiguity, as in marking the difference between:

1   When we arrived at the party the other guests left.
2   When we arrived at the party the other guests had left.

It is therefore difficult, if not impossible, to establish this function without reference to a text or a context. Relying simply on explanation, without examples, places considerable faith in the learners' capacity to create their own contexts. What's more, the teacher compounds the cognitive load by introducing several uses of the past perfect at the same time, again without much in the way of exemplification and using fairly difficult metalanguage to do it with. The only check of the students' understanding is the question *Do you understand?* – hardly a reliable means of gauging the success or not of the presentation.

The practice activity involves a mechanical manipulation, but, in the absence again of much context, there is no way the students could work out what effect on meaning the transformation entails, unless they already knew beforehand. The fact that the practice activity is done individually allows no opportunity for collaborative learning. Nor does the open class check provide students with a high volume of speaking practice. Finally, by switching to an unrelated word game, the teacher misses an opportunity to set up some kind of more language-productive, interactive activity, as a means, for example, of personalising the language. For example:

Use this pattern to write five true sentences about yourself:

Before I _____, I had never_____.

For example:
'Before I went to Brussels, I had never met a Belgian.'

Exchange your sentences with your partner's, and ask each other questions about them. For example:
What were you doing in Brussels?
Was it like you expected it would be?
etc.

In short, the lesson earns low marks for both E- and A-factors. While it was relatively **easy** for the teacher, in that it involved little or no preparation, the failure to use the time available productively to engage the learners, or to provide the minimal conditions for learner understanding, means that the **economy** and **efficacy** of the lesson are less than optimal. The predominantly teacher-fronted approach, plus the lack of any content – such as a text – to stimulate the students' interest, or of any activity that might involve them in real communication, runs counter to the need to provide a motivating classroom environment. This is especially important for learners of this age group (i.e. teenagers), who may have no specific motive for learning English, but who generally respond positively to purposeful, interactive tasks.

In short, the teacher has adopted a teaching-is-transmission approach to the teaching of grammar. In other words, the lesson is based on the belief that simply by explaining the rules of grammar they will magically be internalised. The evidence seems to run counter to this view.

Some rules What conclusions, then, are to be drawn about the teaching of grammar? Here are some rules of thumb:

- The Rule of Context: Teach grammar in context. If you have to take an item out of context in order to draw attention to it, ensure that it is re-contextualised as soon as possible. Similarly, teach grammatical forms in association with their meanings. The choice of one grammatical form over another is always determined by the meaning the speaker or writer wishes to convey.

- The Rule of Use: Teach grammar in order to facilitate the learners' comprehension and production of real language, rather than as an end in itself. Always provide opportunities for learners to put the grammar to some communicative use.

- The Rule of Economy: To fulfil the rule of use, be economical. This means economising on presentation time in order to provide maximum practice time. With grammar, a little can go a long way.

- The Rule of Relevance: Teach only the grammar that students have problems with. This means, start off by finding out what they already know. And don't assume that the grammar of English is a wholly different system from the learner's mother tongue. Exploit the common ground.

- The Rule of Nurture: Teaching doesn't necessarily cause learning – not in any direct way. Rather than occurring as flashes of insight, language learning is more often than not a process of gradual approximation. Instead of teaching grammar, therefore, try to provide the right conditions for grammar learning.

- The Rule of Appropriacy: Interpret all the above rules according to the level, needs, interests, expectations and learning styles of the students. This may mean giving a lot of prominence to grammar, or it may mean never actually teaching grammar at all – in any up-front way. But either way, it is your responsibility as a teacher to know your grammar inside out.

Some conditions

The Rule of Nurture argues for providing the conditions for grammar learning. What are these conditions? If the answer to this much disputed question could be reduced to a handful of essentials, they would probably be these:

- The **input** learners get: will it be presented in such a way that the learners are likely to engage with it, thus ensuring a reasonable chance of it becoming intake?
- Their **output**: will it be of sufficient quantity and/or quality to ensure that they have opportunities to develop both accuracy and fluency?
- The **feedback** they get: will it be of the type and quantity to ensure that some of their attention is directed at form?
- Their **motivation**: will the content and design of the lesson be such that learners are motivated to attend to the input, produce optimal output, and take account of the feedback?

Some caveats

Finally, the teacher – whether new or experienced – is advised to be extremely wary of methodological fashions. Teaching methods come and teaching methods go. And, quite often, they come round again. These shifts in fashion are often powered by dubious theoretical claims that seem to touch a common chord, but which have a shelf-life of a decade or so at best. Teachers' intuitions, on the other hand, that are developed and fine-tuned by years of thoughtful classroom experience, tend to outlive these swings and pendulums. This is not meant to be an invitation to complacency. As professionals, language teachers have a duty to keep themselves abreast of developments in second language acquisition research, in applied linguistics, in educational theory and practice – both inside and outside the domain of language teaching – in fact in any field that has a bearing on language and on learning.

It is reassuring, perhaps, to read the advice opposite, from an English course (*Essential English for Foreign Students, Book Two* by C.E. Eckersley) that was first published half a century ago, and to realise what little, in fact, has changed.

LESSON 5

Parts of Speech

MR. PRIESTLEY: There is a difference between "learning English" and "learning *about* English." Now I want you to learn English, and I believe the best way to learn to speak English is by speaking it; and that is why in our meetings, instead of talking to you about English grammar, I try to get *you* to talk about all kinds of things.

PEDRO: Excuse me, sir, but haven't there been some new ideas in English grammar teaching about "structures" and "sentence patterns"?

MR. PRIESTLEY: Yes, there has been quite a lot of work done, both here and in America, on the structure of English, and next year I'm going to introduce you to those ideas. Some teachers get rather carried away by any new idea and think it is the answer to all their difficulties. In language teaching I don't think this is ever true. A friend once said to me, "You can learn to talk by sentence patterns and 'structure', but you can't learn to write without studying grammar"—and I agree with him; so I'm going to give you from time to time some ordinary straightforward English grammar.

33

Task File

Introduction

- The exercises in this section all relate to topics discussed in the chapter to which the exercises refer. Some expect definite answers while others ask only for the reader's opinions.
- Tutors will, of course, decide when (and if) it is appropriate to use the tasks in this section. Readers on their own can work on the tasks at any stage in their reading of the book.
- An answer key (pages 177–178) is provided after the Task File for those tasks where it is possible to provide specific or suggested answers. The symbol [🔑] beside an exercise indicates that answers are given for that exercise in the answer key.
- The material in the Task File can be photocopied for use in limited circumstances. Please see the notice on the back of the title page for the restrictions on photocopying.

Chapter 1
What is grammar?

 A **Analysing language in terms of chains and slots** Page 2

Here are some sentences in a language you probably won't know, along with their translations in English. See if you can work out the grammar by studying the chains and slots and the translations. Then see if you can complete the sentences (1–5).

	action phrase		subject phrase	translation
	Kei te	mahi	au.	I am working.
	Kei te	oma	au.	I am running.
	Kei te	kai	ia.	He is eating.
1	Kei te	_____	_____	He is working.
2	Kei ____	_____	_____	I am eating.
	Kei te	aha	a Hone?	What is John doing?
	Kei te	moe	a Hera.	Sarah is sleeping.
3	_____	_____	_____	What is Sarah doing?
	Kei te	aha	nga wahine?	What are the women doing?
	Kei te	waiata	te wahine.	The woman is singing.
4	_____	_____	nga wahine.	The women are eating.
5	_____	_____	_____	The women are working.

 B **Which are the well-formed sentences?** Page 2

On the basis of the above, tick the sentences below that are grammatically well-formed, and put a cross by those that are not.

1 Kei te aha te wahine?
2 Kei te kai Hera.
3 Kei te oma ia.
4 Kei aha nga wahine?
5 Kei te waiata ia.
6 Kei te wahine te aha?

☞ **C Different types of grammar rule** Page 11

Put **a**, **b**, or **c** in each box according to whether you think the rule (1–7) comes from:

a   a style guide for writers (hence prescriptive)
b   a grammar of English for linguists (hence descriptive)
c   an EFL students' grammar (hence pedagogic)

1 If you are talking about something that is happening now, you normally use the present continuous: *They're watching TV*. ☐

2 The subjunctive *were* is hypothetical in meaning and is used in conditional and concessive clauses and in subordinate clauses after optative verbs like *wish*. ☐

3 *None* is singular and is therefore followed by the singular form of the verb: *None of us is hungry*. ☐

4 Use a possessive adjective before a gerund: *I was embarrassed by their arriving so late*. Not *I was embarrassed by them arriving so late*. ☐

5 Here are two rules for the order of adjectives before a noun: ☐
   • opinion adjectives usually go before fact adjectives: *this nice old pub*
   • general qualities usually go before particular qualities: *traditional Chinese medicine*.

6 You use *the* when the person you are talking to knows which person or thing you mean. ☐

7 When they have generic reference, both concrete and abstract non-count nouns, and usually also plural count nouns, are used with the zero article: *I like cheese/music/dogs* ... ☐

Chapter 2
Why teach grammar?

A Understanding 'the case for grammar'   Page 15

Read this extract from the *Teacher's Book* for the popular EFL course
Headway Intermediate by John and Liz Soars. Note the arguments that the
writers use, and match these, where possible, with the arguments listed in
chapter 2 under 'the case for grammar', namely:

- The sentence-machine argument
- The fine-tuning argument
- The fossilisation argument
- The advance-organiser argument
- The discrete item argument
- The rule-of-law argument
- The learner expectations argument

Do the writers offer arguments that are not mentioned in the chapter?

The grammar is given such
prominence for several reasons.

1 It is the mechanism that
generates the infinite number
of sentences that we produce and
receive.

_____

2 It is a tangible system, and can
provide one element of a
systematic approach to teaching
a language.

_____

3 It develops students' cognitive
awareness of the language.
Language is rule-based, and
knowledge of the rules is the key
to 'generalizability' and creativity.
Students can do a lot of work on
their own outside the classroom
if the grammar is presented in
clear, digestible portions.

_____

4 It conforms to students'
expectations of language learning,
and meets an often-heard request
for 'more grammar'.

_____

5 It will be of assistance to teachers
in the planning of their lessons.

_____

☞ B Identifying which method your coursebook uses
Pages 21–22

Here are some more extracts (1–5) on the subject of grammar from the introductions to some EFL courses. Can you identify the method in each case? Choose from this list (a–e):

a Grammar-Translation
b Direct Method
c Audiolingualism
d Communicative approach (shallow-end)
e Communicative approach (deep-end)

1 The forms of English are taught, but more important, the rules for their use are also taught – there is little value in learning language forms unless we know when it is appropriate to use them ... Students are encouraged to communicate effectively rather than to produce grammatically correct forms of English.

2 As soon as the pupil has mastered the rules of each lesson, he should learn the corresponding Vocabulary, paying great attention to the spelling of each word. The Dialogues, which are based on the earlier Lessons, will enable him, with the aid of Translation, to learn a variety of idiomatic phrases and sentences, which would otherwise be difficult to acquire.

3 The approach is based on the belief that attention to grammatical structure is essential in language learning, but it does not assume that grammar should therefore be the starting point of learning. The direction, therefore, is from fluency to accuracy ... Students engage in the **Language Activities**. Where a need is identified – either by the teacher or the students themselves – for the target structure, this can be highlighted by drawing students' attention to the appropriate rules.

4 In order to make himself understood the teacher ... resorts at first to object lessons. The expressions of the foreign language are taught in direct association with perception ... The value of the various words and constructions is understood much more easily by means of the practical and striking examples of object lessons, than by the abstract rules of theoretical grammar.

5 The method of presentation rests on the concept that the sentence is the unit of instruction. The framework of the sentence is the structure, a basic pattern constantly expanded by a growing vocabulary ... **Drill and review exercises** have as their primary aim the establishment of habits of automatic language control. It is important that the teacher limit instruction in each lesson to many variations of the same pattern until mastery of that pattern is attained.

Chapter 3
How to teach grammar from rules

☞ A How to identify 'good' rules   Page 32

Look at the following grammar rules (1–6) and assess them according to Michael Swan's criteria (page 32) in the table below. Put ticks and crosses on the grid for each numbered rule

	1	2	3	4	5	6
truth						
limitation						
clarity						
simplicity						
familiarity						
relevance						

1 The choice between *bring* and *take* and *come* and *go* depends on where the speaker is. *Bring* and *come* are used for movement towards the speaker. *Take* and *go* are used for movement away from the speaker.

2 If you want to talk about a past event or situation that occurred before a particular time in the past, you use the **past perfect**.

3 To form the past simple of regular verbs , add *-ed* to the infinitive.

4 *Any* indicates one or more, no matter which; therefore *any* is very frequent in sentences implying negation or doubt (such as questions).

5 A phrasal verb consists of a verb + adverb (e.g. *work out*). The two words form an idiom. It is called a phrasal verb only if the adverb changes the meaning of the verb.

6 As a rule, all sentences in written English (apart from imperatives) have a subject and a verb.

Scott Thornbury *How to Teach Grammar* © Pearson Education Limited 1999
PHOTOCOPIABLE

B How to use a rule explanation Pages 33–38

Plan a presentation along the lines of Sample lesson 1, to teach one of these structures:

1 The active-passive distinction, e.g.:
   a A man bit a dog.
   b A dog was bitten by a man.

2 The difference between direct and reported speech, e.g.:
   a He said, 'I am hungry'.
   b He said he was hungry.

3 The difference between two aspects of the same tense, e.g.:
   a I read a book last night.
   b I was reading a book last night.

C Recognising the overgeneralising of rules Pages 38–41

1 In a language that you know well, think of a grammar area which, like the verb *soler* in Spanish, overlaps in meaning with an English equivalent (*used to*) but is not identical. For example, the **passé composé** in French and the **present perfect** in English:

J'ai déjà reçu l'invitation. = I have already received the invitation.
Elle a été malade la semaine dernière. ≠ She has been ill last week.

2 Design a teaching sequence to 'trap' students into overgeneralising the fit between the two forms. In other words, design an 'up-the-garden-path' sequence similar to the one in Sample lesson 2.

Chapter 4
How to teach grammar from examples

☞ A Selecting example sentences   Pages 51–55

Induction – or working rules out from examples – assumes that students can see patterns in the examples. Here are some sets of sentences. Which sentence is the odd one out in each set? In other words, which sentence does not fit into the pattern? Why?

1   a   The baby's bottle.
    b   The nation's struggle.
    c   The teacher's ill.
    d   The nurse's pay.
    e   The government's defeat.

2   a   The plane was hijacked by a woman.
    b   The tourists were attacked by a gang.
    c   The soldier was hit by a bullet.
    d   The trains collided by a river.
    e   Three hundred people were killed by the earthquake.

3   a   She must have lost the address.
    b   Alan must have been here too.
    c   That must have been awful.
    d   The thieves must have got in through the window.
    e   I must have something to drink.

4   a   I'm not used to the noise yet.
    b   They used to work in a circus.
    c   Didn't there use to be a shop here?
    d   I never used to smoke.
    e   It didn't use to be so dirty.

B Using the Total Physical Response method   Pages 55–57

Devise a TPR (Total Physical Response) lesson for teaching one of these grammatical items:

1   possessive adjectives (*my, his, her, your ...*)
2   verbs that take two objects (e.g. *Give me the ball.*)
3   prepositions of place (*next to, behind, in front of, under* etc.)

C Using realia   Pages 57–59

What 'realia' might be useful for teaching the following grammar points?

1   *some* versus *not any*
2   comparative adjectives
3   possessive adjectives (*my, her, his* etc.)

D Using a generative situation   Pages 59–62

Here is a generative situation. What structure(s) could it be used to teach? What examples could it generate?

> Tom went shopping. First he went to the baker's and bought some bread. Then he crossed the road to the post office and bought some stamps. Then he went next door to the newsagent's and bought a magazine. Then he crossed the road again and had a cup of coffee in a café. When he went to pay, he discovered he didn't have his wallet with his money in it. Now he's wondering where he left it.

E Using minimal sentence pairs   Pages 63–65

Design a set of 'minimal sentence pairs' for each of these contrasts (say, two or three pairs per contrast):

1   present simple versus present continuous.
2   *extremely* + adjective versus *absolutely* + adjective
3   *must have done* versus *should have done*

Chapter 5
How to teach grammar through texts

A Selecting appropriate contexts   Pages 69–72

Which of these two texts provides the better context for presenting *used to*? Why?

1 a: Do you smoke?
      I used to smoke.
   b: Me, too. I used
      to drink, as well.
   a: Let's have an
      orange juice.
   b: That'd be nice.

2 a: Do you smoke?
   b: I used to, but
      I don't any more.
   a: When did you give
      up?
   b: Three years ago.
   a: Why?
   b: I married a
      non-smoker.

B Contextualising example sentences   Pages 69–72

You are planning to teach the first conditional (*If you do X, then Y will happen*) to a class of elementary learners. Write a short dialogue that contextualises examples of this structure. Plan how you would use this dialogue for presentation purposes.

C Finding authentic texts Page 77

The authentic text on page 77 has a high frequency of passive forms. Where might you find authentic texts that have a high frequency of the following grammatical forms?

1 past simple
2 present simple with future reference
3 reported speech
4 imperatives
5 *should* and *must* (for obligation)

D Selecting topics for Community Language Learning
Pages 79–82

You are planning to do a CLL-type activity (see page 81). What topics could you set that might elicit the following structures?

1 *used to*
2 second conditional
3 passives
4 present perfect

E Writing a dictogloss Pages 82–85

Write a text that you could use as a **dictogloss** (see page 82) for the presentation of each of these structures:

1 *going to* (elementary level)
2 third conditional (mid-intermediate level)

Chapter 6
How to practise grammar

☞ **A Choosing activities for accuracy, fluency and restructuring** Pages 91–95

Look at the following activity (from *Headway Pre-Intermediate*).

1 Is it designed for accuracy, fluency or restructuring?
2 How could you adapt the activity to make it suitable for another of the objectives?

---

1 Your teacher will give you a card which begins *Find someone who . . .*

> Find someone
> Who has been
> to Russia.

You must form the question, beginning *Have you ever . . . ?*
Then stand up and ask everyone in the class.

B Using varied drill sequences Pages 95–97

The teacher's plan for the drills in Sample lesson 1 might look like this:

1 *How much milk have we got?* x 6 [imitation drill]
2 *rice, meat, juice, sugar, spaghetti, wine, oil, coffee.* [substitution drill]
3 *How many bananas have we got?* x 6 [imitation drill]
4 *potatoes, eggs, onions, tomatoes, apples, lemons.* [substitution drill]
5 *eggs, meat, coffee, apples, sugar, wine, tomatoes, rice, potatoes ...* [variable substitution drill]

Design a similar sequence to practise the present perfect + *for* or *since* (e.g. *I have been here for three months/I have been here since August.*)

C Designing a task to encourage grammar interpretation
Pages 105–108

Read this short text:

> This year Peter is in Class 2. Last year he was in Class 1. His teacher last year was from Canada. This year his teacher is Australian. There are five students in the class this year. Last year there were 12. This year they are in Room 15. It is not very big. Last year they were in Room 22, which was much bigger. Peter is the only boy in the class: all the other students are girls. Last year there were five boys and seven girls.

Design some true/false sentences that will require learners to interpret the difference between present and past forms of the verb *to be*. For example:

His teacher is Canadian. (False)

(Note that you should try to avoid using time expressions [*last year, this year*] in the sentences, so that the learners' interpretative skills depend entirely on recognising the difference between the tenses.)

D Using conversation in grammar teaching   Pages 108–111

Read this statement:

High frequency grammatical structures, such as the present simple, past simple, and modal verbs such as *should*, *would*, *could* and *might* are fairly easily and naturally contextualised in informal chat.

Choose two of the above grammar items (*should* etc.) and think of ways each could be worked – several times – into a teacher-led classroom conversation.

Chapter 7
How to deal with grammar errors

☞ **A Categorising errors** Pages 114–115

Identify and classify the errors in this text:

> While I was seen my brother I remembered the good moments with him when we were a children. My brother had a long hair and blue eyes. He was very little. He was very unreliable. He always was lost his games. He disliked a lot the school. He said: It's a prison of boys! He liked to climbed some tryes and to play witch his dog. When I was young I hated the dogs. The dog of my brother was black. His name was Blacky. Now, my brother's very tall. He have a long hair because he's a hippy boy.

Are there any errors that seem to be systematic and therefore worth dealing with?

☞ **B Responding to errors**   Pages 117–119

Here is an extract of teacher-learner interaction. Note the different ways the teacher provides feedback (marked →). Can you number them 1–12 according to the list on pages 117–119.

	S1:	What about go to mountains?
a →	T:	What about ...?
	S1:	What about going to mountains, we can do 'barrancking'
		[Ss laugh]
	T:	What's 'barrancking'?
	S3:	You have a river, a small river and [gestures]
	T:	Goes down?
	S3:	Yes, as a cataract
b →	T:	OK, a waterfall [writes it on board] What's a waterfall, Manel?
		Can you give me an example? A famous waterfall [draws]
	S1:	Like Niagara?
c →	T:	OK. So what do you do with the waterfall?
	S4:	You go down.
	T:	What? In a boat?
	S4:	No, no, with a cord.
d →	T:	No, rope, a cord is smaller, like at the window, look [points]
	S4:	Rope, rope, you go down rope in waterfall.
	S2:	You wear ... black clothes ... /espeʃæl kləʊðez/
e →	T:	/speʃəl kləʊðz/ Repeat [student repeats] ... This sounds
		dangerous, is it dangerous?
	SS:	No no
	S3:	Is in summer, no much water
f →	T:	Sorry?
	S3:	Poco ... poco ... little water, river is not strong
g →	T:	OK ... and you have done this? What's it called in Spanish?
	S4:	Barranquismo. In English?
	T:	I don't know. I'll have to ask somebody.

Chapter 8
How to integrate grammar

A Designing a task-teach-task (TTT) lesson
Pages 129 and 132–135

On the opposite page look at a teacher's lesson plan for a PPP-type lesson, designed to teach the comparative form of adjectives. Re-design it so as to turn into a TTT-type lesson.

B Choosing material for a 'tell and record' lesson
Pages 135–137

Look at Sample lesson 3 again. Can you think of a true story of your own that you could use in a 'tell and record' lesson and in to which you could embed examples of either of these:

* indirect speech
* indefinite pronouns (e.g. *somebody, something, anybody, anything, nobody, nothing*)

C Choosing material for a story-based lesson   Pages 138–139

Can you think of another children's story that has a repetitive or refrain-like element that could be used like 'Goldilocks and the Three Bears' with a class of young learners? How would you use this story?

1. Draw figures on board to represent these concepts:
   a. Kim is taller than Chris.
   b. Chris is older than Kim.
   c. Car A is bigger than Car B.
   d. Car B is more expensive than Car A.
   e. Kim is more intelligent than Chris.

2. Elicit sentences a – e. Write up. Highlight form and elicit rule for comparative of short words (tall, old, big) and long words (expensive, intelligent).

3. Exercises to practise:
   a. students write comparative forms of different adjectives: beautiful, fast, rich, comfortable, dangerous, exciting, popular, hot, cool, etc.
   b. students write sentences using above adjectives and based on magazine pictures of e.g. famous cities, famous sportspeople, showbusiness people, modes of transport etc.

4. Students plan holiday in groups of three, choosing between two different holiday destinations, two different times of year, two different modes of transport etc. Choices supplied on cards, e.g.

   go to Istanbul or Cairo?
   go in March or August?
   get there by plane or cruise ship?
   stay in backpackers' hostel or five star hotel?
   rent a car or take public transport?
   go alone or with friends?

Chapter 9
How to test grammar

A Assessing the relative value of tests   Pages 141–143

Here are two more discrete-item tests for *already*, *yet*, *still*. Compare them to the five tests in Chapter 9. How do they rate in terms of control? How effective do you think they are?

1 Complete the spaces with *already*, *yet* or *still*:

a 'Would you like to see the latest James Bond film?'
'No, I've _____ seen it.'

b 'Has Ivan had breakfast?'
'No, he's _____ in bed.'

c 'Can I use your scanner?'
'No, I'm _____ using it.'

d 'Are we late for the film?'
'No, it hasn't started _____.'

e 'Can I clear the table?'
'No, I haven't finished _____.'

2 Complete the sentences, using the word in brackets, so that the meaning is similar to the sentence given:

a I saw this film last year.
[already] I've_____

b Haven't you finished doing your homework?
[still] Are _____ ?

c The train is still in the station.
[yet] The train _____

d We've missed the beginning of the match.
[already] The _____

e I can't remember if you've graduated.
[yet] Have _____ ?
etc.

B Designing a discrete-item test   Pages 141–146

Design short discrete-item tests to test, at elementary level, students' knowledge of:

1 the word order of question forms
2 the difference between the use of *how much?* and *how many?*
3 the use of prepositions of time – *at*, *in*, *on*

C Designing an oral interaction test   Pages 146–149

You have been teaching a group of intermediate students the language of making plans and arrangements. Design an oral interaction task that would test their ability to do this.

D Assessing written compositions   Pages 141–149

Look at this scoring sheet for oral interaction activities from page 147. How could you adapt this so that you could use it for assessing students' **written** compositions?

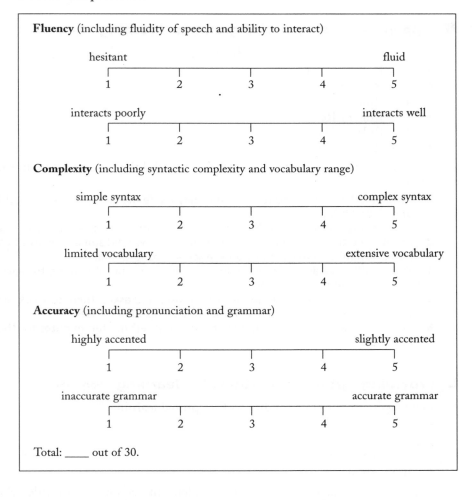

Fluency (including fluidity of speech and ability to interact)

hesitant   fluid

 1   2   3   4   5

interacts poorly   interacts well

 1   2   3   4   5

Complexity (including syntactic complexity and vocabulary range)

simple syntax   complex syntax

 1   2   3   4   5

limited vocabulary   extensive vocabulary

 1   2   3   4   5

Accuracy (including pronunciation and grammar)

highly accented   slightly accented

 1   2   3   4   5

inaccurate grammar   accurate grammar

 1   2   3   4   5

Total: _____ out of 30.

Chapter 10
How NOT to teach grammar

A Improving your teaching   Pages 151–153

Re-design the sample lesson in this chapter so as to make it more effective.
How many different designs can you come up with?

☞ B Applying the six rules of grammar teaching   Page 153

Here again are the six rules for effective grammar teaching.

- The Rule of Context
- The Rule of Use
- The Rule of Economy
- The Rule of Relevance
- The Rule of Nurture
- The Rule of Appropriacy

Here are six teacher 'confessions'. Which rule did the teacher break, in each
case?

1   I explained it and drilled it – and still they made mistakes. So I explained it
    and drilled it again.
2   I taught my business class the present perfect continuous using a fairy tale.
3   I presented the rules of adverb order, and then we did some exercises in the
    book. Tomorrow I'm going to do the second conditional.
4   They don't have any problems with the past tense, but I'm going to teach it
    again because it's in the book.
5   I gave them five sentences in different tenses and asked them to work out
    the difference. Then we did some sentence gap-fill exercises.
6   The presentation took about 40 minutes. That left me ten minutes for the
    role play.

C Providing optimal conditions for learning   Page 154

Here again are the four conditions for optimal learning:

- input
- output
- feedback
- motivation

Examine again the extract of teacher-student interaction in Task File 7B on
page 171. To what extent does this extract show evidence of these conditions?

Task File Key

Chapter 1

A 1 Kei te mahi ia.
2 Kei te kai au.
3 Kei te aha a Hera?
4 Kei te kai nga wahine.
5 Kei te mahi nga wahine.

B 1 ✓ 2 ✗ 3 ✓ 4 ✗
5 ✓ 6 ✗
C 1 c 2 b 3 a 4 a
5 c 6 c 7 b

Chapter 2

B 1 d (from *Building Strategies* by Abbs and Freebairn, Longman, 1979)
2 a (from *The New British Method* by Girau, Magister, 1925)
3 e (from *Highlight Pre-intermediate* by Thornbury, Heinemann, 1994)
4 b (from *Method for Teaching Modern Languages* by Berlitz, 1911)
5 c (from *First Book in American English* by Alesi and Pantell, Oxford Book Company, 1962)

Chapter 3

A Suggested answers:

	1	2	3	4	5	6
truth	✗			✓		✓
limitation		✗	✗			
clarity	✓	✓	✓		✗	✓
simplicity	✓	✓	✓			✓
familiarity				✗	✗	✓
relevance						✓

Notes:
Rule 1: A sentence like *I'll come over to your place* describes movement towards the hearer, not towards the speaker, so the rule lacks truth.
Rule 2: The rule is too broad since it implies that you can't say *I went to the post office and then I went to the bank.*
Rule 3: Unless the students know what the irregular verbs are already, this rule is rather circular – you add *-ed* to verbs except the ones you don't add *-ed* to!
Rule 4: This rule uses terms (*no matter which, negation, doubt*) that may be unfamiliar to learners.
Rule 5: This rule is too limiting, since it excludes non-idiomatic phrasal verbs (e.g. *Stand up, Write it down*), and miscues learners into thinking that idiomaticity (itself a rather subjective idea) is the key issue.
Rule 6: This rule can be particularly relevant for learners in whose own language a subject is not obligatory, e.g. Spanish: *Es profesora* (*[She] is a teacher*).

Chapter 4

A 1 c (The *'s* stands for *is* whereas the others are all possessives.)
2 d (This is an active construction whereas all the others are passives.)
3 e (This has present meaning; the others have past meaning.)
4 a (This means *be accustomed to*. The others mean past habit.)

D Structure: verb forms used to make deductions about the past.
   Examples: *He must have left it in the newsagent's.*
   He can't have left it in the baker's.

Chapter 5

A Text 2, because:
   • *used to* clearly refers to finished habits whereas in text 1 it is not clear.
   • in text 1 *used to* could easily be interpreted as meaning *usually*.
C 1 Narratives (such as fairy stories, jokes, personal anecdotes, narrative songs) history texts, biographies and obituaries
   2 Itineraries (*You arrive in Aswan on the 7th and spend the day sightseeing ...*)
   3 News stories, e.g. reports of court cases and political speeches; statements and complaints (*They said the car was brand new but ...*)
   4 Written instructions, recipes, directions, guide books (*Spend some time in the old town and visit the embroidery museum*)
   5 Regulations (for applying for a driver's licence or visa) and the rules of a game

Chapter 6

A 1 This is a fluency activity.
   2 An accuracy (form) focus could be added by having the students report to the class the results of their survey (*Three students have been to Russia*) for which they prepare by writing sentences first. Restructuring may be assisted by asking students to ask further questions (*When did you go? What was it like?*) which may force them to confront the difference between present perfect (*have you ever ... ?*) and past simple (*when did you ... ?*). (Both these extensions are in fact suggested in the book that the activity comes from.)

Chapter 7

A Vocabulary:
   • Wrong words: *seen*; *little*; *hippy boy*.
   • Wrong spelling: *tryes* instead of *trees*; *witch* instead of *with*.
   Grammar:
   • Wrong word order: *he disliked a lot the school.*
   • Wrong verb form: *was seen*; *was lost*; *to climbed*; *he have.*
   • Overuse of article: *a children*; *a long hair*; *the school*; *some tryes*; *the dogs.*
   • Non-use of possessive forms: *a prison of boys*; *the dog of my brother*
   Systematic errors:
   • Use of *of* where possessive *'s* would be better (*the dog of my brother*)
   • Use of passive forms instead of active ones (*was seen, was lost*)
   • Use of the definite article when no article would be better: *school, dogs.*
B a 5 b 2 c 11 d 9 e 2 f 7 g 11

Chapter 10

B 1 The Rule of Nurture
   2 The Rule of Appropriacy
   3 The Rule of Use
   4 The Rule of Relevance
   5 The Rule of Context
   6 The Rule of Economy

Further reading

The following books are recommended should you wish to consult a grammar reference, or are looking for teaching ideas or simply want to pursue some of the issues raised in this book.

Grammar reference books for students

Murphy, R. (1985) *English Grammar in Use*. Cambridge University Press.
Swan, M. and Walter, C. (1997) *How English Works. A Grammar Practice Book*. Oxford University Press.

Grammar reference books for teachers

Carter, R. and McCarthy, M. (1997) *Exploring Spoken English*. Cambridge University Press.
Collins *COBUILD English Grammar*. (1990) Collins ELT.
Crystal, D. (1988) *Rediscover Grammar*. Addison Wesley Longman.
Downing, A. and Locke, P. (1992) *A University Course in English Grammar*. Phoenix ELT.
Lewis, M. (1986) *The English Verb*. Language Teaching Publications.
Swan, M. (1995) *Practical English Usage (New edition)*. Oxford University Press.

Books about analysing grammar for teaching purposes

Thornbury, S. (1997) *About Language: Tasks for Teachers of English*. Cambridge University Press.
Yule, G. (1998) *Analysing English Grammar*. Oxford University Press.

Grammar recipe books

Hall, N. and Shepheard, J. (1991) *The Anti-grammar Grammar Book: Discovery Activities for Grammar Teaching*. Addison Wesley Longman.
Rinvolucri, M. (1985) *Grammar Games*. Cambridge University Press.
Ur, P. (1988) *Grammar Practice Activities*. Cambridge University Press.

Index